Going Green

by Lydia Bjornlund

LUCENT BOOKS
A part of Gale, Cengage Learning

GALE
CENGAGE Learning™

Detroit • New York • San Francisco • New Haven, Conn • Waterville, Maine • London

GALE
CENGAGE Learning

LIBRARY OF CONGRESS CATALOGING-IN-PUBLICATION DATA

Bjornlund, Lydia D.
  Going green / Lydia Bjornlund.
    p. cm. -- (Hot topics)
  Includes bibliographical references and index.
  ISBN 978-1-4205-0119-3 (hbk.)
  1. Environmentalism--Juvenile literature. 2. Green movement--Juvenile literature. I. Title.
  GE195.5.B56 2009
  363.7--dc22
                                                                        2009008831

Lucent Books
27500 Drake Rd.
Farmington Hills, MI 48331

ISBN-13: 978-1-4205-0119-3
ISBN-10: 1-4205-0119-4

Printed in the United States of America
2 3 4 5 6 7 13 12 11 10 09

Printed by Bang Printing, Brainerd, MN, 2nd Ptg., 12/2009

CONTENTS

FOREWORD

Young people today are bombarded with information. Aside from traditional sources such as newspapers, television, and the radio, they are inundated with a nearly continuous stream of data from electronic media. They send and receive e-mails and instant messages, read and write online "blogs," participate in chat rooms and forums, and surf the Web for hours. This trend is likely to continue. As Patricia Senn Breivik, the former dean of university libraries at Wayne State University in Detroit, has stated, "Information overload will only increase in the future. By 2020, for example, the available body of information is expected to double every 73 days! How will these students find the information they need in this coming tidal wave of information?"

Ironically, this overabundance of information can actually impede efforts to understand complex issues. Whether the topic is abortion, the death penalty, gay rights, or obesity, the deluge of fact and opinion that floods the print and electronic media is overwhelming. The news media report the results of polls and studies that contradict one another. Cable news shows, talk radio programs, and newspaper editorials promote narrow viewpoints and omit facts that challenge their own political biases. The World Wide Web is an electronic minefield where legitimate scholars compete with the postings of ordinary citizens who may or may not be well-informed or capable of reasoned argument. At times, strongly worded testimonials and opinion pieces both in print and electronic media are presented as factual accounts.

Conflicting quotes and statistics can confuse even the most diligent researchers. A good example of this is the question of whether or not the death penalty deters crime. For instance, one study found that murders decreased by nearly one-third when the death penalty was reinstated in New York in 1995. Death penalty supporters cite this finding to support their argument that the existence of the death penalty deters criminals from committing murder. However, another study found that states without the death penalty have murder rates below the national average. This study is cited by opponents of capital punishment, who reject the claim that the death penalty deters murder. Students need context and clear, informed discussion if they are to think critically and make informed decisions.

The Hot Topics series is designed to help young people wade through the glut of fact, opinion, and rhetoric so that they can think critically about controversial issues. Only by reading and thinking critically will they be able to formulate a viewpoint that is not simply the parroted views of others. Each volume of the series focuses on one of today's most pressing social issues and provides a balanced overview of the topic. Carefully crafted narrative, fully documented primary and secondary source quotes, informative sidebars, and study questions all provide excellent starting points for research and discussion. Full-color photographs and charts enhance all volumes in the series. With its many useful features, the Hot Topics series is a valuable resource for young people struggling to understand the pressing issues of the modern era.

INTRODUCTION

ENVIRONMENT AT RISK

Millions of different things live in our world. From the giant blue whale to the tiny ant, from the tallest redwood trees to the tiniest blade of grass, every living thing is dependent on everything else. Going green is about remembering that the decisions we make have an impact on the earth on which we live and the other living things that live here.

Some people say Americans are particularly forgetful of our ecosystem. It is true that Americans use up the earth's resources more quickly than most other countries. The United States has just 5 percent of the world's population, but Americans use about 33 percent of the world's paper, 25 percent of the oil, 23 percent of the coal, 27 percent of the aluminum, and 19 percent of the copper. The United States has roughly 30 percent of the total number of cars and trucks in the world. The average American uses twice as much fossil fuel as the average resident of Great Britain and 2.5 times as much as the average Japanese.

Most of our houses and cars run on fossil fuels. Fossil fuels include coal, oil, and natural gas. These fuels are formed from plants and animals that lived hundreds of millions of years ago. They took millions of years to create—and it would take hundreds of millions of years for today's plants and animals to create new fossil fuels. For this reason, they are considered nonrenewable resources. Many people believe that we need to stop—or at least greatly reduce—the use of these nonrenewable resources and look for other ways to run our cars, homes, and businesses.

People believe that nonrenewable resources should be protected as much as possible. These resources can be conserved in many ways. Turning off lights and appliances that are not in use is perhaps the simplest thing one can do. But going green involves going beyond these simple practices. Some people are implementing new renewable sources of energy. These include solar power, which creates energy from the sun; hydroelectric energy, which is powered by moving water; and wind energy.

The fossil fuels that power America include coal, oil, and natural gas. Here, coal is brought to the surface at a coal mining operation in Pennsylvania.

Fossil fuels are not the only resources that green advocates are trying to protect. They also focus on conserving water. Again, going green involves taking shorter showers and turning off the water when brushing one's teeth. It also means making sure that pipes are not leaky. Some people go beyond these measures by putting in systems to catch rainwater and treat it for use in the house or use it to water their gardens.

Going green also involves protecting the land and its resources. Advocates of green living suggest that people think about where they build their homes and communities, preserving enough open space to support different ecosystems. Pollution may kill plants that animals need for survival. As a result, pollution can threaten entire animal species with extinction.

Pollution

Pollution happens when part of the environment is poisoned or harmed by human activity. Most pollution in the atmosphere is caused when people burn fossil fuels to produce energy. This energy is used to run cars, trains, airplanes, and other vehicles. It is also used to power our homes, businesses, factories, and cities. When fossil fuels burn, they release smoke and invisible gases such as carbon monoxide and nitrogen dioxide. These gases stay in the air, causing pollution.

Air pollution can have a devastating effect on life. It can make people sick. Many people also believe that air pollution is a major factor in global warming. *Global warming* is a term used to describe a worldwide trend that shows that climates are heating up. In some places, such as in Antarctica and on snow-capped mountains, higher temperatures are causing ice to melt. Scientists worry that the melting of the polar ice caps may reduce the habitat of polar bears and other arctic animals, putting them at risk of extinction.

Pollution of any kind disturbs the ecosystem. Ecosystems are delicate systems that support a variety of life forms. Any impact on one part of an ecosystem can affect all other parts of it. If people pollute a marsh, for instance, the plants and animals that live there may get sick. Some animals might not survive. If one species of plant or animal dies out, the other plants and animals

Air pollution blankets the Santiago, Chile, skyline in 2008. Air pollution has a huge negative effect on ecosystems.

that depend on that species might also die. In the end, the entire food chain may be affected.

Going green means avoiding pollution and poisons in our environment. Although this might seem obvious, many poisons have widespread and important uses. Farmers spray their crops with pesticides to kill bugs that eat crops, for instance. These pesticides are poisonous to other bugs and animals, not just the ones that destroy crops. When farmers spray crops with pesticides, some falls onto the ground. When it rains, the rain carries the pesticides into our waterways. Gradually, these pesticides may build up in a waterway until they harm the fish or other life that lives there.

Many people believe that it is unhealthy to eat foods sprayed with pesticides or other chemicals. They avoid these foods and choose to eat organic foods, which have not been treated with chemicals. Some people believe organic foods are better for people and the environment. Similarly, green consumers may look for shampoos, soaps, and other health and beauty products made from organic ingredients and wear clothes made only from organic cotton, wool, or silk.

Pesticides are just one of the ways pollution can happen. Many of the paints, glues, and cleaning fluids that are common in homes across America also are toxic, or poisonous, to some forms of life. Many people are going green by trying to rid their homes—and their lives—of these toxins.

Garbage

People are also concerned about the amount of garbage thrown out each year. Almost everything we touch eventually becomes garbage. The clothes we wear, the newspapers and magazines we read, the toys and electronic games we play—more than three-quarters of this waste is dumped in huge holes in the ground called landfills. When one landfill gets full, another one is opened to hold new garbage.

Many people believe landfills create an environmental hazard. One problem is that some types of waste in landfills ooze into the ground, creating a liquid called leachate. Leachate can cause pollution in surrounding areas. Landfills also sometimes create air pollution. Some materials emit a gas called methane as the garbage decomposes, which happens when chemicals break down into smaller or more simple pieces. Some scientists say that methane is a strong greenhouse gas that contributes to global warming. Other household products found in landfills give off VOCs, or volatile organic compounds, which also pollute the air. Landfills also sometimes contain products with mercury and other chemicals that are bad for the environment.

Some environmentalists have targeted landfill waste as a major concern. They separate out materials that can be reused or recycled by grinding them up and making something new out of them. People can also separate food scraps, yard waste, and other biodegradable materials. Biodegradable materials are made of substances that decay relatively quickly, breaking down into elements such as carbon that are recycled naturally. Through a process called composting, green consumers make these materials into a rich substance that can be used to condition soil and fertilize plants.

Green consumers also try to reduce the amount of waste by buying less and using less packaging. Green advocates pay particular attention to avoiding the use of nonbiodegradable materials, such as plastics. Nonbiodegradable items never rot, so they will stay in landfills forever.

We all have an impact on the earth. It is impossible to completely erase our carbon footprint or reach the ultimate goal of

A tractor moves garbage at a landfill. Many people believe landfills create environmental hazards such as air pollution and leachate runoff.

zero waste. But people can make a difference. Even minor changes to daily habits—such as taking a shorter shower or turning off lights that are not being used—can protect valuable resources. Many people are making more substantial changes to their lives to help protect the environment. They walk or bike where they need to go; they power their homes with solar or wind power; they grow their own organic foods. In myriad ways, an increasing number of Americans are recognizing the need to do what they can to preserve and protect the earth and its resources for future generations.

WHY GREEN?

In a 2006 poll, 90 percent of Americans said they were concerned about the environment. People also said they engaged in some green practices to help protect the environment. Sixty-seven percent of respondents said they purposely cut down on the amount of electricity or gas they use at home; 62 percent recycle cardboard, newspaper, glass, and/or plastic; and 53 percent looked for ways to cut back on their use of water.

The poll also showed that Americans are willing to spend more money on "green" products. Organic food—which is grown without pesticides or artificial fertilizers—tends to cost more than other food. Still, more than one-third of Americans said they buy organic food a "fair" or "great" amount of the time. Almost 70 percent of Americans use lower-energy lightbulbs, which cost five times more than regular incandescent bulbs but use less energy. (According to industry analysts, an average 60-watt lightbulb costs $.42, versus $2.99 for a low-energy lightbulb that provides the same light.) These lower-energy bulbs also last much longer than incandescent bulbs.

People often look for other ways to reduce the amount of energy they use. In a 2007 poll, nearly nine out of ten people said they would switch to products and services that produce lower greenhouse gas emissions. Two-thirds said they would be willing to pay a higher price—11 percent more, on average—for these products and services.

Some people *say* they want to pay extra for green solutions, but they continue to choose cheaper options. Thus, the most successful green measures are usually those that help the environment *and* save people money. Hybrid cars, for example, are a greener choice than traditional cars because they use less gas and cause less pollution. But hybrids cost more than other

In an effort to go green, many people are replacing their old (incandescent) lightbulbs with high-efficiency compact fluorescent lightbulbs (CFL).

cars. Some people have bought hybrids anyway, because they are willing to pay extra to help protect the environment. Today, the high price of gas is fueling demand for hybrids because many people believe their fuel efficiency will save them money in the long run.

What Does It Mean to Go Green?

"Going green" means different things to different people. To some people, it means switching to a car that uses less gas. To others, it means getting rid of the car altogether and walking or biking wherever they need to go. When some people think of going green, they focus on what they buy. They buy only organic groceries and carry their goods home in reusable bags. They might also buy second-hand items or cut back on the amount of things they use. Others think of going green as furnishing their home with the latest energy-saving devices and appliances.

Earth Day

In the 1960s, there was little concern for environmental issues. Cars ran on leaded gas, smoke billowed from factory smokestacks, and many companies dumped toxic waste into America's waterways. April 22, 1970—the first Earth Day— marked the beginning of a change.

Earth Day 1970 took its cues from the protests Americans were staging to fight for civil rights and to oppose the Vietnam War. Organizers held rallies across America. An estimated 20 million Americans took part, coming together to demonstrate their commitment to the environment.

Over the past four decades, Earth Day has evolved. The message of Earth Day changes as environmental needs and priorities change, but the goal remains the same: to call attention to environmental issues. Today, as in 1970, people come together each April 22 to celebrate the earth. Educators and environmentalists use Earth Day as a reminder not only of what the earth has to offer, but also of our responsibility for caring for it.

Today, the Earth Day Network is stronger than ever. More than a half

billion people participate in Earth Day Network campaigns every year. Earth Day's international network reaches more than seventeen thousand organizations in 174 countries; the U.S. program engages five thousand groups and more than twenty-five thousand educators coordinating millions of community development and environmental protection activities throughout the year.

Earth Day volunteers clean a beach in Panama City, Panama. Earth Day takes place every year on April 22.

Many people do these things without considering themselves green. They conserve energy to save money. They recycle glass, aluminum, and plastic because their local government requires them to. But other people do these things as part of an ongoing effort to reduce their impact on the environment. Going green is an important part of their lives.

The Media Spread the Word

From a very young age, people are taught to take care of the world around them. Popular children's shows such as *Sesame Street* routinely include stories about saving water and electricity, recycling, and trash control. The science curriculum in most elementary schools includes information about pollution, energy, and global warming. Many elementary schools also sponsor poster or essay contests about issues of environmental concern. Some schools also initiate hands-on learning opportunities in which students track the amount of trash they generate, plant organic gardens, engage in recycling programs, compost food waste, or find creative new uses for common materials that would otherwise be thrown away.

POLLS SHOW SUPPORT FOR THE ENVIRONMENT

"Solutions to the key environmental challenges are available, achievable and affordable, especially when compared to the expected economic growth and the costs and consequences of inaction." —Angel Gurria, secretary general of the Organization for Economic Cooperation and Development, which includes thirty countries committed to democracy and the market economy.

Quoted in "OECD: Tackle Environmental Problems Now or Pay More Later," peopleand planet.net, March 10, 2008, http://www.peopleandplanet.net/doc.php?id=3224.

Adults, too, are bombarded with information about how to go green. Popular books offer many suggestions for how to reduce waste and where to buy green products. An Internet site called TreeHugger has developed more than one hundred guides "to help you green your lives with ease."[1] The site contains guides

Actor Ed Begley Jr. stands in the backyard of his "green" home, which is equipped with solar heating panels on the roof, a solar oven, and a water recycling system.

on greening everything from gardens, houses, and pets to weddings and funerals. Similarly, National Geographic has an online "Green Guide." The site provides tips on green travel, green entertainment, green remodeling, and many other topics. Mainstream media also showcase people who are working to help the environment and green projects. *Time* magazine, for instance, offers a weekly column on the topic. Many sites have started on the Internet where people come together to discuss the challenges of going green, offer tips, and share information about new products.

Living green is also a popular topic for TV shows. HGTV's *Living with Ed*, for instance, a reality show that follows Ed Begley Jr. and his wife, Rachelle Carson, as they try to go green. The popularity of the show has spawned a book and Web site of the same name.

In the summer of 2008, the Discovery Networks launched Planet Green. This is the first channel focused exclusively on going green. Network spokespersons explain that they are trying to appeal to people who would like to help the environment but do not want to put a lot of effort into it. "We want to engage people in a fun way and in the spirit of what we can all do together,"[2] says David Zaslav, the head of Discovery Networks.

One of the new shows on Planet Green is called *Battleground Earth*. On the first episodes, Ludacris, a rapper, competes against

Hollywood Goes Green

A number of Hollywood actors and actresses have used their fame to lobby on behalf of the environment. Ed Begley Jr. is one of Hollywood's most committed environmentalists. He drives an electric vehicle, owns a solar-powered home, and has his own brand of eco-cleaners called Begley's Best. He also stars with his wife in an HGTV program called *Living with Ed*, a reality show that follows Begley and his wife as they try to go green. "I think all citizens have a responsibility to get involved, but with celebrity, you have an added responsibility," says Begley. "You need to seek out the best science and get your facts straight before you ever approach a mike or a camera."

Several other young Hollywood actors have followed Begley's lead. Academy Award–winning actor Leonardo DiCaprio has championed environmental issues for many years. Through the Leonardo DiCaprio Foundation, he has spread awareness of environmental issues and produced two short films: *Global Warning* (2003) and *Water Planet* (2005). In 2007, he coproduced, cowrote, and narrated an environmental documentary called *The 11th Hour*. To further emphasize the warning set out in this documentary, DiCaprio set up an environmental Web site (leonardo.dicaprio.org). The Web site calls attention to environmental issues and trends such as the ongoing effort to cease the use of plastic bags.

Edward Norton has focused his attention on reducing the waste involved in making movies. Norton also created the BP Solar Neighbors Program, which aims to lower energy costs for poor families in Los Angeles by converting their homes to solar power.

Quoted in Michael Ventre, "Walking the Talk: Some Celebs Are Living Green," msnbc.com, April 22, 2008. www.msnbc.msn.com/id/24052164/.

Tommy Lee, a rock singer, in a series of green challenges such as solar-powered racing and building a home from bamboo, which is generally considered a greener product than wood. Another show, *Alter Eco*, starring eco-friendly actor Adrian Grenier, aims to inspire people to find better, greener ways to do things. Grenier explains that the purpose of the show is to get people to understand how they can make small changes in their life. "The main focus is how to be creative when you're trying to do things you want to do anyway,"[3] he says. Early episodes of the show include a tour of an eco-friendly winery; the complete environmental renovation of a home in Los Angeles, California; the transition of a nightclub to a restaurant serving organic foods; and a surprise visit to a busy family striving to be kinder to the planet.

NO ONE WANTS TO PAY

"It's a funny thing about being environmentally friendly: everybody's in favor of it, but nobody wants to pay more for it." —Bob Pietrangelo, a chemical industry executive.

Quoted in Steven Ashley, "It's Not Easy Being Green," in *Scientific American: Critical Perspectives on Environmental Protection*, ed. Krista West. New York: Rosen, 2007.

The Real Story

Several moving documentaries about the environment have also been aired in recent years. In 2006, Keanu Reeves and Alanis Morissette told about global warming and environmental activism in *The Great Warming*. Tom Hanks starred in a 2006 documentary called *Who Killed the Electric Car?* that tells the story of the EV1, an electric vehicle introduced in the 1990s. In 2008, the National Geographic Channel aired a four-part series called *Strange Days on Planet Earth*, which explores the environmental challenges facing the earth.

Perhaps the best-known documentary on the environment is *An Inconvenient Truth*, which hit theaters in 2006. In the movie, former vice president Al Gore warns people of the devastating effect that global warming will have if it is unchecked. "The world won't 'end' overnight in ten years," Gore says. "But a point

In the documentary An Inconvenient Truth, *former vice president Al Gore warns people about the devastating effects of global warming.*

will have been passed, and there will be an irreversible slide into destruction."[4]

An Inconvenient Truth was a surprise hit. It won many awards, including the 2006 Academy Award for Best Documentary Feature. More important to Gore and others involved in making the movie was its impact on the American public. It spurred a new group of people into action. "What can we do?" asked movie critic Roger Ebert in a review of the film. "Switch to and encourage the development of alternative energy sources: Solar, wind, tidal, and, yes, nuclear. Move quickly toward hybrid and electric cars. Pour money into public transit, and subsidize the fares. Save energy in our houses. I did a funny thing when I came home after seeing *An Inconvenient Truth*. I went around the house turning off the lights."[5]

An Inconvenient Truth helped motivate many people to be more environmentally conscious. Yet, as in many environmental issues, the film's accuracy was questioned. Scientists were especially critical of its dire message. Many questioned the science in the movie. The movie claimed that the earth was growing hotter and that the 1990s had witnessed the highest temperatures in history. Two British scientists issued a scientific report showing the opposite—that the earth has in fact been cooling. Other scientists say that global warming is part of the earth's natural cycle and question Gore's claims that it is caused by—or even influenced by—people. Most scientists agree that Gore exaggerated some of the claims in the movie. "I don't want to pick on Al Gore," says Don J. Easterbrook, professor emeritus of geology at Western Washington University in Bellingham, Washington. "But there are a lot of inaccuracies in the statements we are seeing, and we have to temper that with real data."[6]

From One to Many

Although the earth may not be in imminent danger, as some claim, making efforts to reduce waste and live more consciously can help. Choosing to go green used to be a personal decision that required effort. Twenty years ago, most Americans thought little about throwing everything into the trash, for instance. According

Recycling is encouraged in many communities. Bins are often provided for recycling purposes and are picked up at the curb to make recycling as convenient as possible for people.

to the U.S. Environmental Protection Agency (EPA), there was only one curbside recycling program in the United States, which collected several types of recyclable material at the curb. The few people who thought to recycle had to take their recyclables to one or more collection centers. These recycling centers, usually located on the outskirts of town, were hard to find. Sometimes they were open a few hours a day, and many collected just one kind of material. Some required people to sort and clean their recyclables. Paper, glass, and aluminum had to be separated. Some centers also required glass to be sorted by color. Although these measures helped the centers reduce costs—and therefore made recycling economically feasible—it made recycling inconvenient for individuals.

GOING GREEN IS NOT EXPENSIVE

"Most people believe that 'going green' is a luxury, an expensive choice that they can't afford. What if I told you that going green doesn't have to be expensive—and, in fact, you can go green and SAVE money—and if you invest green you can get RICH?" —David Bach.

David Bach, with Hillary Rosner, *Go Green, Live Rich: 50 Simple Ways to Save the Earth and Get Rich Trying.* New York: Broadway Books, 2008.

In contrast, recycling is encouraged in most places today. According to the EPA, by 2006, about 8,660 curbside programs had sprouted up across the nation and more than five hundred facilities had been established to process the collected materials.

To encourage people to comply with recycling rules, some local governments provide bins for sorting recyclables and carrying them to the curb. In addition to paper, cans, and plastic, some local governments hold special collection times for yard waste, Christmas trees, and used appliances.

It is also easier than ever for consumers to find green products. Organic foods have made their way from specialty stores into most supermarket chains. Manufacturers of everything from paint to furniture to clothing to beauty products are responding to the demand for green products with a wealth of products made from organic and natural materials.

Greenwashing: Is Green Always What It Seems?

In order to appeal to the growing number of green consumers, more businesses are selling green items. Some companies also exaggerate their "greenness." They may change the name of a product, create packaging that indicates a product is natural, or emphasize a product's organic materials in its advertising or promotional materials.

Today's grocery shelves are stocked with "natural" potato chips, "natural" cheese puffs, and "organic" chewy chocolate chip bars. But if you look closer, you can see that these so-called

Although many foods are labeled "natural," true organic food is sold under the organic seal and produced using the organic system, free from additives such as preservatives, pesticides, and antibiotics.

natural products sometimes include preservatives, food dyes, and other ingredients. Even those made with organic ingredients are not necessarily healthy. As one consumer says, "If you fry an organic potato, it's still a French fry."[7]

These junk food manufacturers are engaging in practices called greenwashing. Greenwashing describes the act of pretending to be green just to look good. Greenwashing companies mislead consumers about the benefits of their brands, products, and services.

In 2006, an environmental marketing firm called Terra-Choice randomly surveyed 1,018 common consumer products, ranging from toothpaste to shampoo to printers. Of these products, 99 percent were promoted using some form of green washing. Scot Case, vice president of TerraChoice, uses the example of a shampoo with packaging that promised a "totally organic experience" but included "zero evidence that the product contained any organic ingredients." Many "organic" or "natural" beauty products contain fossil fuels. "We saw absolutely ridiculous claims. And vague, too. What the heck does 'earth-friendly' mean?"[8]

OUR IMPACT ON THE EARTH

"Many people today assume mistakenly that the Earth is so big that we humans cannot possibly have any major impact on the way our planet's ecological system operates. That may have been true at one time, but it is not the case any more. We have grown so numerous and our technologies have become so powerful that we are now capable of having a significant influence on many parts of the Earth's environment." —Al Gore, former vice president and Nobel Prize–winning environmentalist.

Al Gore on Environment, On the Issues, www.ontheissues.org/celeb/Al_Gore_Environment.htm.

"Consumers are inundated with products that make green claims," adds Scott McDougall, the president of TerraChoice. "Some are accurate, certified and verifiable, while others are just plain fibbing to sell products."[9]

Men in Yangon, Myanmar, cart bamboo to a building site. All over the world, bamboo has become a popular material for flooring and furniture because of its sustainability.

Environmental Trade-Offs

The most common greenwashing technique TerraChoice found is what it calls the "sin of the hidden trade-off." This happens when a manufacturer emphasizes a relatively minor green aspect of a product while ignoring other, more damaging impacts on the environment. Lexus, for instance, flew a new hybrid sport utility vehicle (SUV) from Japan to Paul McCartney in England. The purpose of a hybrid is to reduce fossil fuel consumption and air pollution. Critics said that it used far more fuel to fly the car

ENERGY STAR

Several government agencies and non-profit organizations are working to pave the way for the environment. ENERGY STAR, for instance, is a joint program of the U.S. Environmental Protection Agency and the U.S. Department of Energy. The purpose of the ENERGY STAR program is to encourage the use of energy-efficient products and practices. Through the program, the federal government labels products in more than fifty product categories, including computer equipment and household appliances. The ENERGY STAR label is used for products that work as well as comparable models while using less energy.

Programs like ENERGY STAR work because people know that energy-efficient appliances are better for the environment and can save them money in their electric bills. Therefore, they look for appliances with the ENERGY STAR label.

halfway around the world than will ever be saved by its hybrid engine.

Critics also blame the bottled water industry for greenwashing. Many bottled water companies emphasize the "naturalness" of the water, ignoring the fact that the plastic bottle is damaging to the environment. A lot of energy goes into bottling the water. And the plastic is nonbiodegradable—it will remain in landfills forever. Of course, no company wants to remind consumers of the damaging effects its products have on the environment.

The automobile offers another example. Carmakers often market their new, "green" vehicles. But critics say that creating a truly green car is impossible. All cars pollute. All cars require energy, metals, and raw materials when they are made. Just because one car uses fewer resources than another does not make it green.

The entire green movement is involved in greenwashing of sorts, say critics. They argue that the costs of going green often outweigh the benefits. Take recycling, for example. Trucks are needed to collect the recyclables; these trucks burn fossil fuels and pollute the air. Energy is also needed to sort and clean recyclables. Cleaning the recyclables sometimes also uses a considerable amount of water. Sometimes the detergents used to clean recyclables runs off into waterways, polluting the water. Special equipment may be needed to keep harmful waste products from escaping into the air, water, and soil—further resources are needed to create and power this equipment. Even where recycling rates are high, many of the potential recyclable materials end up in the waste stream because no one wants to buy them.

Carbon Offsetting

Another questionable practice is something called carbon offsetting. The basic idea of carbon offsetting is figuring out how an individual contributes to global warming through such activities as driving, flying, or using energy. This is a person's carbon footprint. People "erase" their carbon footprint by buying carbon offsets, which fund activities that reduce greenhouse gas emissions. For instance, some programs might pay for wind farms, which produce clean energy to replace fossil fuels, or the planting of forests, which provide trees to help clean the air. When a person buys 10 tons of carbon offsets, for instance, the seller guarantees that 10 fewer tons of global warming pollution go into the atmosphere.

IS GLOBAL WARMING REAL?

"Global Warming, as we think we know it, doesn't exist. We are wasting time, energy and trillions of dollars while creating unnecessary fear and consternation over an issue with no scientific justification." —Timothy Ball, chairman of the Natural Resources Stewardship Project and former climatology professor at the University of Winnipeg, Manitoba.

Timothy Ball, "Global Warming: The Cold, Hard Facts?" Canada Free Press, February 5, 2007. www.canadafreepress.com/2007/global-warming020507.htm.

Carbon offsetting is a relatively new approach, but it has rapidly gained popularity. In 2006, about $91 million in carbon offsets were purchased.

People or organizations can purchase carbon offsets for one trip or event. The band Maroon 5 offset carbon emissions for its 2007 U.S. tour by contributing $1.00 from every ticket sold to an organization called Global Cool, which uses the money to support a variety of "planet-saving" projects. In 2007, the Academy Awards purchased carbon offsets as part of its effort to be "carbon neutral." Promoters of the Super Bowl and NASCAR races have also claimed to have carbon-neutral events.

Some companies offset their greenhouse gas emissions for the entire year. Stonyfield Farms, for instance, offsets 100 percent of the carbon dioxide emissions from its facility. It has used some of the offsets to fund a program called Climate Counts. This program helps measure companies' contributions to global warming. Climate Counts can help green consumers know which companies contribute the least to global warming and identifies areas in which companies can improve their practices.

Carbon-Offsetting Programs

A number of programs have emerged to help people calculate their carbon footprint and pay to compensate for this footprint. Some offsets are better than others. With so many options to choose from, it can be confusing for people to figure out how to best offset their use of energy.

Tufts Climate Initiative conducted a study of carbon-emission offset programs. The following programs invest in the most effective projects and are the most accurate in terms of calculations.

- Native Energy (www.nativeenergy.com) invests in wind power and methane gas energy production facilities on U.S. family farms.
- Atmosfair (www.atmosfair.com) develops solar power in developing countries and methane entrapment in Thailand.
- My Climate (www.myclimate.org) funds solar greenhouses in the Himalayas, biomass facilities in India, and farms in Madagascar.
- Climate Friendly (www.climatefriendly.com) puts money into renewable energy in Australia and New Zealand.

Not everyone believes that carbon offsetting is a good idea. Critics say that it is impossible to quantify how much of an offset a project generates. Kevin Smith, a researcher at the research organization Carbon Trade Watch, says carbon offset programs require people "to speculate on a fantasy scenario"[10] in which they guess what it costs to pollute the environment with any given activity.

NEW ENERGY SOURCES ARE NEEDED TO FIGHT GLOBAL WARMING

"What we need to combat climate change is a complete transformation of our energy system, and that requires a lot of new stuff to be built and installed, some of it in places that are relatively untouched." —Stephen Tindale, executive director of Greenpeace UK.

Quoted in Heather Timmons, "A Renewable Source, and Clean, but Not Without Its Critics," *New York Times*, August 3, 2006, p. C1.

People also worry that carbon offsetting encourages people to continue to engage in activities that are harmful to the environment. In a *BusinessWeek* article titled "Another Inconvenient Truth," author Ben Elgin writes, "Rather than take the arduous step of significantly cutting their own emissions of carbon dioxide, many in the ranks of the environmentally concerned are paying to have someone else curtail air pollution or develop 'renewable' energy sources."[11]

Some people who have studied offsetting programs say that there is no way to know whether the money organizations have received for carbon offsets has really made a difference. *BusinessWeek* studied six programs that had received funds from carbon offsets. Five of the six said the offsets had not played a significant role in their decision to cut emissions. Offsets went to the utility company in Catawba County, North Carolina, which turned gas from its landfill into electricity. "It's just icing on the cake," says Barry Edwards, director of utilities and engineering in Catawba County. "We would have done this project anyway."[12]

Making Green Choices

Clearly, going green is not as simple as it appears. Consumers need to carefully consider the claims made by manufacturers. For those who want to go green, greenwashing presents a problem. It is sometimes difficult to know which options are best for the environment.

Several programs and organizations have emerged to help with this problem. ENERGY STAR, which is used primarily for appliances, and LEED certification for buildings are two familiar programs. Products that carry their certification have met certain energy-saving standards. Consumers can also look for green labels on products. EcoLogo and Green Seal are two such examples. Both of these programs look at the entire life cycle of a product, from the materials used to create it to what happens

Green labels on products and programs such as ENERGY STAR and LEED have emerged to help people decide what products are better for the environment.

to it when it is disposed of. In addition, an organization called EnviroMedia has created a Web site where consumers can rate the green claims made by companies.

Many organizations are making it easier than ever for Americans to minimize their impact on the earth, but it still takes individual initiative. Municipal governments pick up recyclables in far greater quantities than ever before, but it requires families and households to separate their recyclable materials from the rest of the trash, take them to the curb or recycling center, and buy the products made from these recycled goods. With the many claims of companies trying to capture the attention of "green" consumers, it also depends on individuals to learn and understand what programs and products are best for the environment.

GREEN ON THE GO

Ellen McRae, a real estate agent in Falls Church, Virginia, needs a car for work. "I cannot ask clients to walk or take a bus to the houses they want to see," she says, "but I can cut back on the amount I use my car when I'm not showing houses." McRae lives in a suburban area where most people drive where they want to go. But she prefers to walk. "I often walk to the library, the post office, and the park, which are all less than a mile from where I live," she explains. McRae also has three children at three different schools. "My kids' schools are also within walking distance. They ride the school bus, but I often walk when I'm volunteering there."

Like other people, McRae does not only have the environment in mind when she chooses to walk. "I have a dog that lives to walk. I find myself looking for places to walk so I can take him with me," she says.

In 2008, McRae bought a scooter for trips that are just a little too far to walk. "I found myself taking the car when I was in a hurry or for trips to the supermarket. The market is just a little too far to walk. And it can be hard to tote the groceries home. Now, I take the scooter. It uses more gas than walking, but just a fraction of the gas I'd use if I drove. I realize that I'm not going to save the world, but I'm glad to be able to do my part."[13]

Walking and Biking

The easiest way to go green is to get out of the car. According to the U.S. Department of Transportation, American adults drive 15 million miles every day for trips that are only a half mile or less—a distance it would take just ten minutes to walk. All this driving burns valuable fossil fuels and contributes to air pollution.

In addition to providing a healthier environment, walking provides a healthier lifestyle. Lois Fletcher lost thirty pounds when she stopped using her car and began riding the transit system in Atlanta instead. She walked four or five miles a day, including up and down the stairs. "In my old office, the parking garage was right there," she says. "I could park 30 feet from my desk. I have diabetes and high blood pressure, and my doctor would say if you would just walk for 30 minutes, that would really help, but I could never find the time to do it. With three boys, when I got off work, the last thing I thought about was exercise."[14]

Biking is also gaining popularity as a green mode of transportation. To appease the growing number of people who bike daily to school, to work, or on errands, bike manufacturers are producing lightweight bikes that are easy to store. Some bicycles have a headlight that is powered by pedaling, a rack for carrying a briefcase or other essentials, and even a cup holder for coffee or bottle of water. Some bikers are fitting their bikes with electric motors that supply more power when needed. Electric bikes enable people to go farther and navigate hilly roads.

Actor Tate Donovan loves biking. He rides his bike any chance he can get. He has even ridden it to awards programs in

The Hybrid Is Born

At the 1995 Tokyo Auto Show, Toyota demonstrated a futuristic hybrid concept vehicle, which consisted of an electric motor connected to a regular gasoline engine. Toyota called its car the Prius.

At the time, the concept of a hybrid was viewed as idealistic at best. Toyota believed in its car, however, and introduced it in Japan in 1997 and in the United States in 2001.

Toyota sold more than one hundred thousand Prius hybrids in the United States in 2007 and expected sales to increase by 50 percent in 2008. Vehicle owners say they know why. The 2008 Prius gets 45 miles per gallon on the highway. The U.S. Environmental Protection Agency says it is the most fuel-efficient car on the road today.

A bicycle lane in downtown Seattle, Washington. With more people biking to work, cities are increasing the number of biking-only lanes on the roads.

Hollywood. "With the weather, there's no excuse for not riding a bike in L.A.," he says. But he admits it can be dangerous. "People actually yell at me for being on my bike."[15]

Biking around some cities—like Los Angeles—can be dangerous. Some people who drive say they would prefer to walk or bike, but there are no sidewalks or bike paths where they live. Developers are starting to hear their concerns. New "walkable" neighborhoods are being designed to encourage people to walk. Planners are also making bike trails on old railroad tracks or paths that telephone or utility companies have paved to lay their lines.

Strength in Numbers

Walking or biking might not be practical for longer trips. Some people ride buses, subways, or trains to get where they need to go. The savings is in the numbers; with more people riding together, there is less fuel and less air pollution per person. William W. Millar, president of the American Public Transportation Association (APTA), agrees. "Riding public transportation is one of the most powerful weapons Americans have in combating global climate change,"[16] he says.

Still, many communities are not well served by public transportation. And in some places where people can take the bus or train, it is inconvenient. Some people also think the fares are too

Using public transportation helps fight global warming because it uses less fuel and produces less air pollution per person.

high. As a result, fewer than 5 percent of Americans routinely use mass transit systems to get to and from work. Fewer still use it for shopping, errands, or visiting friends. A *Wall Street Journal* editorial sums up the criticism: "There are just two problems with mass transit. Nobody uses it, and it costs too much."[17]

Pooling Resources

Where public transportation is unavailable or inconvenient, people sometimes carpool to school or work, joining with others who are headed their way. In some places, private businesses

Carpool lanes help ease pollution and traffic congestion in locations where they are in use.

have helped encourage carpooling by providing message boards or other networks for people to find would-be riders or drivers who live in their area. Vanpooling has emerged as another option. Some companies lease or buy vans and designate one of the employees to drive or have employees rotate driving responsibilities.

CARBON DIOXIDE DANGER

"Pump enough CO_2 [carbon dioxide] into the sky, and that last part per million of greenhouse gas behaves like the 212th degree Fahrenheit that turns a pot of hot water into a plume of billowing steam." —Jeffrey Kluger.

Jeffrey Kluger, "The Tipping Point," *Time*, April 3, 2006, p. 35.

Wyeth Pharmaceuticals, a large drug manufacturer, has been recognized by the EPA for its efforts to reduce its impact on the environment. The company's Commuter Assistance Center coordinates transportation and commuter programs made available to more than thirteen thousand employees at its sites. The center matches employees by residence, work hours, and office location for carpool and vanpool groups, and a free shuttle service for employees transports mass transit riders from public transportation centers to work. Each month, participants in the program save almost a million miles of driving and close to forty thousand gallons of fuel.

Another strategy is to combine trips. Rather than taking several trips and returning home after each one, green consumers run all their errands on the same day. This is an easy way for people to cut back on the number of miles they drive and reduce their carbon dioxide emissions.

Cleaner Fuels

Driving less is not the only way to reduce pollution. Drivers can also choose cleaner fuels for their cars. Biofuels, for example, are made from plants. Ethanol is the most common biofuel. Ethanol is usually made from corn, but it can also be made from wheat, sugar, or sorghum. Usually, ethanol is mixed with gasoline. E85—a combination of 85 percent ethanol and 15 percent conventional gasoline—is generally less expensive than gasoline, delivers slightly more horsepower, and gets slightly lower fuel mileage. Experts say that powering a car with E85 reduces greenhouse gas emissions by as much as 70 percent.

Biodiesel is another biofuel. Biodiesel is derived from refined vegetable oils such as soy, canola, and recycled restaurant grease. Biodiesel can be used in any car or truck with a diesel engine. Usually, 20 percent biodiesel is mixed with 80 percent diesel—a formula called B20. Country singer Willie Nelson has his own line of biodiesel fuel called BioWillie, which is made from 100 percent vegetable oil. B20 reduces carbon emissions by 30 percent. Commercial biodiesel may be more expensive than regular diesel or gasoline, but the fuel economy is significantly better. And like other biofuels, it is biodegradable.

BIOFUEL AT HOME

"There is really no need going around starting wars over oil. We have it here at home. We have the necessary product, the farmers can grow it." —Willie Nelson, country singer and maker of BioWillie.

Quoted in Matt Curry, "Willie Nelson's New Gig: Biodiesel," MSNBC, January 14, 2005. www.msnbc.msn.com/id/6826994.

Actress Julia Roberts is among the enthusiastic spokespersons for alternative fuels. When she was pregnant with twins, her husband gave her a vehicle that ran on biodiesel for her birthday. (She already owned a Toyota Prius, a hybrid that runs on gasoline and electricity, but she needed a bigger car.) "It's very important that we expand our use of clean energy and make a long-term commitment to it," says Roberts. "Biodiesel and ethanol are better for the environment and for the air we breathe."[18]

Another fuel alternative is propane, which is usually used for gas barbecues and camping stoves. In March 2008 the Yellow Cab Company in Las Vegas, Nevada, announced that it

Using cleaner fuels in cars helps reduce pollution. Experts say that using E85, which is a combination of 85 percent ethanol and 15 percent conventional gasoline, reduces greenhouse gas emissions by as much as 70 percent.

was converting some of the cars in its fleet to run on both gasoline and propane. "Propane burns more cleanly than gasoline," explains a Yellow Cab spokesperson. "The converted propane cabs are said to run 15 to 20 mpg [miles per gallon] farther than non-converted cabs with one-half the [carbon dioxide] emissions."[19]

Many communities also are trying to reduce the carbon footprint of city streetcars, trains, and buses. Some have converted their fleets to run on natural gas, which burns more cleanly than other fossil fuels. Others are using biofuels. "Public transportation is a green industry and transit agencies are working to make it greener,"[20] says Millar. For example, in 2008, the metro bus company in St. Cloud, Minnesota, introduced a bus powered by recycled deep-fryer vegetable oil. The light rail line in Minneapolis, Minnesota, uses wind energy to power its trains.

One of the main disadvantages of these newer fuels is that they are sometimes hard to find. One driver of a car that runs on compressed natural gas writes, "For most people, it isn't really a big deal if you start running low on fuel in your gasoline-powered car. Unless you're in a few remote places, a gas station is likely only a few short miles away. That's not the case with our Civic GX. [From here], the nearest CNG fueling stations are

Hypermiling: Getting Farther on One Tank of Gas

When it comes to protecting the environment, how you drive may be as important as what you drive. As part of the effort to improve gas mileage, a new trend called hypermiling has emerged. Hypermiling is all about making adjustments to maximize gas mileage, regardless of whether a person is driving a hybrid or a Hummer. "Anybody can be a hypermiler," says Wayne Gerdes, who averaged over 90 miles per gallon driving a Honda Insight. "It doesn't matter if you're in a Dodge Durango getting 10 mpg today. You can get 15 mpg tomorrow. It's going to save fuel. And this country needs that."

Tips for improving energy efficiency include driving slower. For every 5 miles per hour above 55, most cars lose about 10 percent of their fuel economy. Avoiding quick starts and sudden braking also helps. Another thing green drivers keep in mind is that the best route may not be the shortest route. A route that is less hilly and has fewer stoplights may help conserve energy. Car maintenance can also help improve fuel mileage. For instance, keeping tires properly inflated can improve gas mileage by about 3 percent.

Quoted in Joshua Zumbrun, "How to Increase Your Gas Mileage," *Washington Post*, August 6, 2006, www.washingtonpost.com/wp-dyn/content/article/2006/08/03/AR2006080301403_2.html.

either at a public utility . . . about 25 miles away or in the industrial outskirts of Hartford (30 miles away)."[21]

People also worry that growing corn and other crops for fuel is taking land that should be used for food. A June 2008 article in *Newsweek* contends that biofuels "have driven up the cost of food without doing much to slice emissions."[22] Some researchers agree that growing crops for biofuels uses up too much land. Scientists are looking for other fuel options, including an ethanol fuel made from farm waste.

FOOD OR FUEL?

"It is now abundantly clear that food-to-fuel mandates are leading to increased environmental damage. First, producing ethanol requires huge amounts of energy—most of which comes from coal. Second, the production process creates a number of hazardous byproducts, and some production facilities are reportedly dumping these in local water sources. Third, food-to-fuel mandates are helping drive up the price of agricultural staples, leading to significant changes in land use with major environmental harm." —Lester Brown, founder and president of the Earth Policy Institute, and Jonathan Lewis, a climate specialist and lawyer with the Clean Air Task Force.

Lester Brown and Jonathan Lewis, "Ethanol's Failed Promise," *Washington Post*, April 22, 2008, p. A19.

Hybrids

"I was raised at the tail end of the 1950s, when environmental activism was born," says Joe Morra, a government attorney who lives in Rockville, Maryland. "Concern for the environment has been instilled in me my whole life. I recycle. I plant trees. I am a member of the Wildlife Fund. I view owning a car as a necessary evil."[23] Like most Americans, Morra cannot simply give up his car, so he decided on a hybrid.

Hybrid cars run on both gasoline and a battery pack. Hybrids run on gasoline at high speeds, but switch to the battery at low speeds or when stopped—at a red light, for instance. This offers

The electricity port of the Ford Edge hybrid. Experts predict that 11 percent of the cars sold in 2013 will be hybrids, compared to just 2.5 percent in 2008.

a more fuel-efficient and cleaner option. According to some experts, hybrids get much better gas mileage. The Toyota Prius, for instance, gets an estimated 50 miles per gallon in the city. Even the smallest cars running on gas usually do not get more than 30 miles per gallon.

Today's hybrids cost about $4,500 more than other cars, but many people are willing to spend the money because they think the gas savings will make them less expensive in the long run. The authors of *The Green Book* estimate that the average driver of a hybrid saves more than twenty gallons of gasoline a month. "If an additional 1 percent of vehicles sold in the United States [in one year] were hybrids, the gasoline saved would fill nearly 4,600 tanker trucks,"[24] the authors contend.

"With gas above $4 a gallon, hybrid cars are hotter than a laptop battery,"[25] writes Keith Naughton in *Newsweek*. In addition to individual drivers, taxi companies and rental car companies are looking at hybrids to reduce their operating expenses. Manufacturers are coping with the growing demand by coming out with new models. In 2005, Ford introduced the first hybrid sport utility vehicle. Experts predict that 11 percent of the cars sold in 2013 will be hybrids, compared to just 2.5 percent in 2008. "By then, we'll have 89 hybrid models from which to choose," writes Naughton, "up from 16 today."[26]

Hybrids are particularly fuel efficient in city driving because they switch to battery mode when idle. This may be one reason for their popularity in Los Angeles, a city known for its traffic. One reporter writes: "The list of Hollywood's hybrid-come-lately car owners reads like headlines on the cover of *People Magazine:* Cameron Diaz, Leonardo DiCaprio, Carole King, Billy Joel, David Duchovny, Patricia Arquette, Jackson Browne and Bill Maher, to name-drop a few. Larry David purchased three, including one for his character, 'Larry David,' to drive one on his HBO series, 'Curb Your Enthusiasm.'"[27]

GOING ON THE GREEN RIDE

"The green, sustainability movement is going mainstream, and we want to ride that wave." —Steve Case, founder of AOL and investor in alternative vehicle projects.

Quoted in Annys Shin, "Internet Visionaries Betting on Green Technology Boom," *Washington Post,* April 18, 2006, p. D1.

Not everyone is convinced that hybrids are the green solution of the future, however. The Toyota Prius, the first hybrid, gets a 50 percent efficiency boost from its hybrid technology, but other hybrids get just 10 percent or less. In fact, the Union of Concerned Scientists says that half of all hybrid vehicles currently on the market are no more fuel efficient than their non-hybrid versions.

Electric Vehicles

As the name implies, electric vehicles are powered by electricity. Usually, the vehicles are equipped with battery packs that can be recharged by simply plugging the car into a wall socket. Many electric vehicles are prohibited from highways because they cannot go faster than 35 miles per hour, but they have become popular ways to get around the neighborhood.

Electric vehicles generate 60 percent fewer greenhouse gas emissions than gasoline-powered vehicles. In addition to protecting the environment, electric cars cost less to operate. Steve Heckeroth of the American Solar Energy Society says that electric cars cost roughly 2 cents per mile, compared to at least 20 to 30 cents per mile for vehicles fueled by gasoline, ethanol, or biodiesel.

The biggest obstacle to electric vehicles is that most cars cannot travel very far before they need to be recharged. With a list price of more than $100,000, the Tesla Roadster—a top-of-the-

The Tesla Roadster, an electric sports car, can go 220 miles on a single charge but carries a list price of over $100,000. Less-expensive cars go far less than 220 miles on one charge.

line electric sports car—can go 220 miles on a single charge, but more affordable cars stop at less than half this range. Charging the car usually requires simply plugging it into a socket. Some environmentalists also point out that most electric cars get their power from electric companies, most of which still depend on fossil fuels.

Hydrogen Fuel Cell Vehicles

Hydrogen fuel cell vehicles are not yet available on the market, but some automotive experts say that they are the answer to America's future fuel needs. One of the best things about hydrogen-fueled vehicles is that they produce only water, so they emit no greenhouse gases. Hydrogen is readily available; in fact, it is the most abundant element in the universe.

CARMAKERS ARE NOT AS GREEN AS THEY SEEM

"The environmental rhetoric coming out of the last two years of 'eco' auto shows does not reflect true vehicle production. The industry's goal has been to fool consumers into believing that automakers are producing eco-conscious cars. Nothing could be further from the truth." —Jodie Van Horn, spokesperson for Rainforest Action Network.

Quoted in Global Exchange, "Michigan Students to Rally for Green Cars Not Greenwashing at Detroit Auto Show," press release, January 10, 2008.

The main problem with hydrogen fuel cells is that it takes a lot of energy to separate the hydrogen from other molecules. In addition, the technology is very expensive.

Still, early models prove promising. The Public Works Department in the city of Burlington, Vermont, uses a Toyota Prius that has been converted to run on hydrogen fuel cells. Evermont, a hydrogen research facility in Burlington, built a station to supply the fuel. Several American automakers have test cars on the road. If these test cars do well, they may be available for sale in the next couple of years. "Developing a viable automobile powered by a hydrogen fuel cell has progressed from a distant dream to a vision that's being achieved in real time," writes Ron Cogan, the editor of the *Green Car Journal*. "The ability to buy vehicles with better environmental performance today allows drivers to make real-time contributions to a better world, every mile they drive."[28]

Air Travel

The advances that have come to automobiles are far from completion in airplanes. In her 2008 book *Gorgeously Green*, Sophie Uliano calls flying "an environmental nightmare."[29] Today, air travel is responsible for roughly 2 percent of total carbon emissions worldwide. Experts predict this number will grow to 10 to 17 percent of emissions by 2050 because more people will be flying. According to Dan Imhoff, author of *Paper or Plastic*, an airplane's takeoff uses the same amount of energy as 2.4 million lawnmowers running for twenty minutes. Uliano adds that flying is much worse than driving "because the toxic chemicals that are spewed out are much closer to the ozone layer—they go straight in, whereas on the ground, many of them evaporate on their way up."[30]

Two percent of carbon emissions are caused by airplanes. Many "green" millionaires are trading in their private jets, like the Cessna Citation X pictured here, and are electing to fly commercial.

No matter how much people love the environment, they might be unable to simply give up flying. Many Americans live on one coast and work or have family on another. Others have jobs that take them to other places in the world. An increasing number of Americans who are concerned about the environmental costs of flying are buying carbon offsets to make up for the polluting effects of flying. Delta was the first U.S. airline to participate in a carbon offset program. Passengers who buy tickets on Delta's Web site can add $5.50 to offset their travel. Delta donates the money to the Conservation Fund, a national nonprofit conservation organization that plants trees.

HYDROGEN ENERGY IS POSSIBLE

"Hydrogen is a pathway to a sustainable energy future. Achieving this goal, however, will require significant new energy security and environmental policy actions in addition to technological developments." —Mike Ramage, chairman of a National Research Council panel on alternative fuels.

Quoted in MSNBC, "Hydrogen Future Doable, Experts Tell Congress," July 17, 2008. www.msnbc.msn.com/id/25719194.

Some people believe that carbon offsetting programs like Delta's will do little to address the world's environmental woes. Joe Romm, an expert who has testified before Congress on carbon offsets, says that carbon offsetting gives people the idea that all they have to do is plant a few trees to make up for air pollution when they fly. "It's very unproductive to leave people with the impression that we could possibly plant our way out of the problem,"[31] he says.

Scientists at Boeing, the National Aeronautics and Space Administration (NASA), and elsewhere are looking for ways to make airplanes greener. In the meantime, many Americans are planning to cut back their air travel. Green millionaires are choosing to travel by commercial airlines rather than hiring their own private jets. As with cars and other ground transportation, the fewer people who are on each plane, the more fuel that is used per person. People with more modest incomes are doing

The Smart Car

The Smart Car achieves energy efficiency mainly through its size. At just eight feet, eight inches long, the Smart Car is so small that it can be parked nose to the curb in a standard parallel-parking stall. Manufactured in Europe by Mercedes and Swatch, it was introduced in the United States in early 2008.

The Smart Car attracted immediate attention with its cute form and fuel efficiency. The basic model starts at less than twelve thousand dollars, and more than thirty thousand people had paid a deposit before the first car came off the assembly line.

Matt Day, a resident of Juneau, Alaska, replaced his Jeep Wrangler with a Smart Car in February 2008. According to owner Day, the Smart Car has reduced his gas consumption by 75 percent. "It gets the highest mileage of any car I know of," Day told a reporter for the *Juneau Empire*. As he looked out the window at the SUVs lining the highway, he added, "There must be a lot of rich people in Juneau."

Quoted in Greg Skinner, "Going Green: Juneau Drivers Think Up Inventive Ways to Save Gas," *Juneau Empire*, June 15, 2008, www.juneauempire.com/stories/061508/loc_291124474.shtml.

This Smart Car gets forty-one miles per gallon on the highway and thirty-three in the city.

their part by spending their vacations closer to home so they do not need to take a plane at all.

Imagine a life without cars, trains, or airplanes. Imagine having to walk or bike everywhere you needed to go. Air pollution would be reduced. Fossil fuels would be preserved. But this future vision is unrealistic. People rely on cars, trains, airplanes, and public transportation to get to school and to their jobs. They travel by car or bus to visit family and friends across town and across the country. They fly to other parts of the world to seek out new experiences, learn about other cultures, and help less-fortunate societies.

Automakers, engineers, and scientists are making great progress in finding greener ways to travel. Until solutions can be found, green consumers will continue to find ways to reduce their own carbon footprints.

THE GREEN HOUSE

In 2004, Steve Glenn, a business leader who founded a computer software company, set out to build the greenest home in America. By combining building materials, energy-efficiency measures, and a sprinkle of ingenuity, Glenn succeeded in creating what *BusinessWeek* called the "Greenest House on the Planet."[32]

Many of the house's green aspects deal with energy efficiency. Rather than air conditioning, for instance, a "whole-house" ceiling fan is used to provide a steady breeze. Water for sinks and showers is heated by solar heat, captured by a panel of glass tubes on the roof. The heated water is also used under the floor to heat the home. The solar heating system is more energy efficient. On sunny days, the home gets enough power from the sun to meet over 80 percent of its power needs. Natural landscaping is also used to keep the house cool in the summer and warm in the winter. Double-pane glass is used for windows and sliding doors to further improve energy efficiency. Glass walls provide a lot of light during the day, reducing the use of electric light.

Glenn's home also conserves water. Rainwater is collected from the roof and yard for use in the home. Then, this same water is collected as it runs from sinks and showers. The used water—called gray water—is used to water the lawn. The house includes a roof garden, which the gray water also waters.

Other measures to keep the home healthy include the use of steel and concrete. Unlike wood, these materials are not affected by mold and termites. The paint used in the home is free of toxic fumes.

Glenn says the eco-friendly features added about 20 percent to the base cost of the home. He estimates that he will save about $1,500 a year on utility bills. This means he will not make up the difference in cost soon, but Glenn says the point is to live in a home that causes the least damage to the environment.

Glenn hopes that others agree. In 2006, he started a business called LivingHomes that sells houses based on his model. All the parts of a LivingHomes house are made in a factory and then shipped and assembled at a homeowner's site.

The Impact of Buildings on the Environment

Glenn has capitalized on the green movement's interest in creating homes that are less damaging to the environment. "I believe that buildings are far and away the worst thing humans do to the environment," said Rob Watson, a scientist with the Natural Resources Defense Council (NRDC). "The built environment devours half of all the world's material and resources, half of all

The home of former vice president Al Gore in Nashville, Tennessee, has earned the U.S. Green Building Council's second-highest rating for sustainable design.

forests. . . . Think about all the toxins produced in the mining of materials, the air pollution, the chewed-up land. No other human activity even comes close to this kind of impact."[33] Buildings also consume a lot of energy. "Buildings use twice as much energy as cars and trucks," says Watson. "Seventy percent of the electricity in the United States is consumed by our homes and our office buildings."[34]

Architects, developers, builders, homeowners, and others have sought to address these problems through green building. Although the methods green builders use vary considerably—and the resulting buildings vary even more—the goals typically include conservation of natural resources in building materials and ongoing energy requirements, the improvement of indoor air quality, and the reduction of environmental impacts.

So what is green and what is not? To help identify how green a building is, the U.S. Green Building Council created a rating system called the Leadership in Energy and Environmental Design, or LEED. LEED provides guidelines for sustainable building in five key areas: sustainable site development, water savings, energy efficiency, materials selection, and indoor environmental quality. Architects, developers, builders, and others often use LEED standards to help them reduce the impact of their projects on the environment.

GREEN SHOULD NOT BE SO HARD

"Green design is getting easier, but doing the right thing shouldn't be so darn hard. Industries should be required to do the research and to provide unbiased information, so architects can select products that work from the traditional standpoint of beauty, cost, and durability, and just compare environmental impact numbers across products. We need to keep encouraging the building industry to be more responsible so we don't have to be so smart." —Jason McLennan, an architect and author of several books on architecture and sustainable design.

Quoted in Cheryl Weber, "The Green House Effect: Eco-Friendly Design Grows More Practical and More Acceptable," *Residential Architect*, March 2005. http://findarticles. com/p/articles/mi_m0NTE/is_2_9/ai_n13609545/pg_2.

The Hotel Industry Goes Green

To attract the business of eco-friendly consumers, many hotels in the United States and abroad are implementing measures to go green. The Kimpton Group, for instance, has incorporated green principles into its operations. Each of its hotels features water conservation and recycling programs and nontoxic cleaning programs. Organic coffee and wine are among the options for guests. The Hotel Triton in San Francisco, a Kimpton property, has even more extensive green practices. Guests can stay in the Red Hot Chili Pepper Suite, equipped with used furniture, hemp textiles, and organic cotton sheets, or in the Woody Harrelson Room, which has bamboo floors.

Fairmont Properties, which operates luxury hotels, began a Green Partnership program in 1990. Since then, bathrooms have been retrofitted with low-flow showerheads, toilet dams, and tap aerators to conserve water, as well as energy-efficient lighting. Every front desk computer in every hotel runs on certified wind energy. The Fairmont Chateau Lake Louise draws 40 percent of its energy from wind power and hydropower. The Chumbe Island Coral Park is in a protected area of Tanzania mandated to have zero impact on the environment. It uses solar water heating and electricity, rainwater catchment systems, and composting toilets.

The National Association of Home Builders, a trade association representing home builders and remodelers, also has created a voluntary residential green building program called NAHBGreen (www.nahbgreen.org). The program includes a free online scoring tool, national certification, industry education, and training.

Governments also are getting in on the green movement. Across America, government buildings—from city halls to police stations, from county courthouses to public housing developments—are being built according to strict environmental standards. In 2005, Washington became the first state in the United States to enact green building legislation. According to the law, all major public buildings, including public schools, are required to meet or exceed LEED standards in construction or renovation. The state estimates that this measure will save 20 percent in energy and water costs, 38 percent in wastewater, and 22 percent in construction waste.

Location and Siting

The first step in green building is to consider the entire landscape when deciding where to build. One of the goals of green development—whether a single house or thousands of acres—is to preserve as much of the natural environment as possible. Green developers avoid cutting down trees and filling in wetlands. Some cluster houses together on one part of the land so the rest can be preserved as trails, parkland, forest, or even a working farm. Prairie Crossing, a renowned conservation development with 356 homes just forty miles north of Chicago, Illinois, includes a ninety-acre farm that produces organic vegetables, fruit, flowers, and eggs for residents and the surrounding public.

PULLING IT ALL TOGETHER

"A key mistake is not taking a global view of what green building is. People focus on health issues, supply chain issues, design issues—but you need to look at all of these things together."
—Steve Thomas, a resident at Planet Green, a green educational media resource owned by the Discovery Networks.

Quoted in Matt Woolsey, "Nine Earth-Friendly Fixes for Your Home," *Forbes*, April 14, 2008. www.forbes.com/2008/04/14/green-home-energy-forbeslife-cx_mw_0414realestate.html.

Green developers also site buildings so they take advantage of the landscape. They use the sun, wind, trees, and vegetation to provide heating, cooling, lighting, ventilation, and shade. Experts say that in cold climates, orienting a building along the east-west axis, so the long side of the building faces directly south, can save 25 percent on heating bills. In warmer climates, green developers position windows and walls to maximize breezes and use awnings and trees to help shade windows from the sun.

The size of the home also matters. Larger houses have a larger footprint. They take up more land, leaving less room for plants, trees, and animals to live. They use more building materials. They also require more energy to heat, cool, and light. "If you have a family of three it's ridiculous to be in a 5,000-square-foot house because you can't recover the energy resources," says one green builder. "You could put in the greenest everything, but you'll never catch up if the house is too big."[35]

Building Materials

A green building starts with materials that have low impact on the earth. Some green building materials are renewable and can be grown organically. Bamboo has become a popular building material. Bamboo is in fact a grass, not a wood, but when woven together it is very strong. Bamboo grows quickly—stalks can grow one hundred feet in just six years. When harvested, the stalks are cut down but the root system remains intact, enabling the bamboo to regrow quickly. For this reason, bamboo is generally considered a sustainable option.

Many building materials can be used that have a low impact on the earth. Straw bales can be used to insulate homes, like this straw bale home in Crestone, Colorado.

Cork is another popular green option for flooring. Because cork comes only from the bark of the tree, it can be harvested without having to cut down the tree. The bark usually grows back in six to nine years, with no harm to the tree itself. Cork has the additional advantage of providing good insulation, protecting homes from both the summer heat and the winter cold.

Still, all choices have trade-offs. Some people say that bamboo is not as green as some people think. Most bamboo comes from China. To meet the growing demand for bamboo, Chinese companies are cutting down old-growth forests to make way for bamboo plantations. In addition, it requires significant energy to transport the bamboo from China all the way to the United States. Top-quality cork has the disadvantage of being hard to find and thus sometimes expensive. As a result, many builders continue to rely on other wood products.

When new wood is used, green builders make sure that wood is taken from a certified sustainable forest. The Forest Stewardship Council (FSC) was created in 1993. It certifies forests that are managed to support the growth of new trees. The FSC label on furni-

The Benefits of Trees

Trees help the environment in many ways. Trees help clean the environment of toxic gases, even in urban areas, where there is much more concrete than trees. In New York City, for example, 5 million trees help remove toxins from the air. New York City's trees are estimated to save taxpayers $10 million a year they would otherwise have to spend to address air pollution.

Trees also help to shade homes and buildings, making them cooler and more energy efficient. In some urban areas, major shade trees cool surface temperatures between 9 and 13°F. The shade from trees also reduces people's exposure to harmful sun rays. Large pines and other evergreens are sometimes planted to block winter winds, reducing the amount of energy used for heating. Because leaves from trees keep rain from falling as quickly, trees also help reduce storm water runoff. Trees also provide habitat for birds, squirrels, and a host of other animals that bring life to urban neighborhoods.

ture and other wood items ensures that these products are made from wood grown in forests that support sustainability principles.

Some green builders also look for local materials. The closer building materials are to the site of the building, the less energy is required to transport them to the building site. Bill Grater, an architect in Clayton, New York, includes local materials whenever possible for his clients' houses. He used stones from an old quarry on Oak Island, in Hammond, New York, for walls and fireplaces for two clients who built summer homes there. Using local materials not only makes environmental sense, it also makes sense aesthetically. Houses made from local stones and other building materials blend better with the surrounding landscape.

GREEN BUILDING FOR EVERYONE

"A lot of the high-profile green projects that get builders' attention are very high-end, but the simple fact is that there are plenty of strategies for inexpensive green building, from right-sizing the structure to optimal value engineering to reducing waste, among many others." —Alex Wilson, president of BuildingGreen Inc. and executive editor of *Environmental Building News*.

Quoted in Rob Fanjoy, "Busted! Eight Green Building Myths," HGTVpro.com. www .hgtvpropicks.com/hpro/nws_ind_nws_trends/article/0,2624,HPRO_26519_ 4953809,00.html.

Recycled materials are another green choice. One office building in Missouri has floors made from recycled rubber. A building at the Vermont Law School uses recycled plastic for bathroom partitions.

Reclaimed materials, which are taken from structures that have been torn down, are even better than recycled options. Wood, tiles, bricks, or stone can be taken from houses or other structures when they are torn down. "Whenever we can reuse a product instead of producing a new one from raw materials— even if those raw materials are recycled—we save on resource use and energy,"[36] explains one author. Not only does using reclaimed materials save the cost of creating new ones, it also saves building materials from demolished sites from going to the landfill. In

2000, a company called Alberici decided to build its headquarters on a site that contained a three-story brick office building. Rather than demolishing the building and starting over, the company reused most of the materials in the building in its new facility, saving 97 percent of the materials from the landfill.

Television star Adrian Grenier lives in a Brooklyn, New York, home that he rebuilt with green principles in mind. He used reclaimed oak for the floors and recycled blue jeans for insulation. The Ranch House in Del Sur, California, which recently received the highest LEED rating possible, also uses reclaimed materials. Rocks found at the site were used to build a chimney and fireplace, and planks from a demolished barn were used for the floors. Sunflower shells were ground up and made into cabinets. Like Grenier's house, the Ranch House is insulated with cotton fibers and shredded scraps of blue jeans.

Some building materials are readily available and inexpensive. Homes throughout the Midwest farmland are built of stacked wheat straw bales—a readily available agricultural product. Straw bales also can be a great source of insulation. Some homes also make use of recycled newspapers for insulation.

With creativity, the options are endless. Manufacturers offer kitchen and bathroom countertops made from a variety of recycled materials, including recycled glass, paper, or aluminum. Homeowners have used the bottoms of wine bottles for glass partitions in their bathrooms or a backsplash for their range. For a more rustic look, they might use branches stripped of their bark for porch railings.

Enhancing Energy Efficiency

When people think of conserving energy, they often think of turning off lights and other appliances when they are not in use. But conserving energy begins long before this. Selecting the appropriate building materials in the first place can do far more to conserve energy than all of the things a person can do to try to save energy afterward. In fact, researchers indicate that state-of-the-art energy-efficient houses require only about 25 percent as much energy for heating and cooling as most existing houses. Although such houses can cost thousands more to build, they

A man stands next to his polyurethane hard cell insulated home. Well-insulated homes conserve energy and can save up to 30 percent on heating and cooling costs.

save money on fuel and electricity expenses in the long run. Households that use ENERGY STAR products save an average of $600 a year in energy costs. A recent state of California study reported that 2 percent additional cost in a green building's design translates into savings of up to 20 percent in energy costs over the life span of the building.

Not all energy-efficiency measures require a lot of money. Improving energy efficiency begins by strengthening the protection from outdoor elements. This begins with proper insulation in walls, ceilings, and floors. Well-insulated homes can save up to 30 percent on heating and cooling costs. High-efficiency windows with double-pane glass and low emissivity can further accomplish this goal.

Tinted windows, awnings, and carefully planted trees that take advantage of natural shade can make a house cooler in warm climates. Even paint color can make a difference. Houses in the southern part of the country tend to be lighter because lighter colors reflect more sunlight than darker ones.

Green homeowners can also save energy by installing ceiling fans, thermostats that are set to heat or cool different rooms according to when they are in use, and dimmer switches. They may keep the water temperature on their water heater at a lower level and perhaps install a timer to efficiently heat the water when it is needed. Going green also involves making decisions about when and how to use appliances: running the dishwasher or washing machine only when it is full, for example. Some green consumers include monitoring systems to help them find out how much energy they are using and what they are using it for. At the Westcave Preserve Environmental Learning Center in Round Mountain, Texas, for instance, a monitoring system continually displays the amount of energy that is being used compared to what is generated from the solar panels on the roof.

Daylighting

Windows are important to energy-efficient buildings for several reasons. Windows that open to let in fresh air can save money on air conditioning, particularly if they allow cross-breezes from one side of the house to another. Well-placed windows also can help save energy otherwise needed for lighting a room. Daylighting is a technique used to maximize natural light, so less electricity is needed to light the building during the day. In addition, because daylight generates less heat than lightbulbs, daylighting can also save on the amount of energy needed to cool a space.

A Carbon-Neutral Building

In 2007, the Aldo Leopold Foundation headquarters in Fairfield, Wisconsin, became the first LEED Platinum "carbon-neutral" building. The building uses a solar electric system to produce 15 percent more energy than it uses. Proper insulation and a design that allows for daylighting and cross-ventilation help the building achieve its lofty energy-efficiency goals. Among the other green features of this very green building is the use of sustainable timber for almost 100 percent of its structure and the recycling of gray water from sinks for use in flushing toilets and landscaping. The toilets also have a local dual-flush option, which uses different amounts of water depending on the amount of waste. "The building does things that people are dreaming about," said Rick Fedrizzi, president of the U.S. Green Building Council. "There are people out there saying, 'Somehow, somewhere a building will be able to do that.' This building is doing it today."

Quoted in Jorge Chapa, "First LEED Platinum Carbon Neutral Building!" Inhabitat, November 8, 2007, www. inhabitat.com/2007/11/08/first-leed-platinum-carbon-neutral-building.

The Aldo Leopold Foundation in Fairfield, Wisconsin, became the first LEED Platinum "carbon-neutral" building.

While many well-lit spaces include a lot of windows, experts emphasize that daylighting depends not on the number of windows but rather on where they are located. According to the Daylighting Collaborative, "Good daylighting technique depends on the proper placement of windows and performance characteristics such as visible light transmittance and solar heat gain coefficient—not having large amounts of glass."[37]

Daylighting strategies may include using skylights, atriums, sloping ceilings, and other design features to eliminate dark corners. Researchers estimate that daylighting techniques used for the Lockheed Missiles & Space Company's office building in Sunnyvale, California, has reduced lighting energy use by about 75 percent compared to a conventional building.

Many public buildings and schools also use motion detectors that automatically turn off the lights when people are not there. Green homeowners also install motion detectors on their

Windows are very important in energy-efficient buildings. At this Giant Eagle grocery store in Brunswick, Ohio, electric illumination is regulated by the amount of sunlight captured through the skylights, saving energy.

outside lights, automatically lighting up the pathway to the front door when needed. This saves people from having to keep lights on when they are out at night.

Electricity savings can also be found by installing dimmers that allow people to use less wattage when bright light is not needed.

Alternative Energy

Some builders avoid the problem of energy efficiency altogether by installing renewable energy sources right at the site. Other builders are capitalizing on the power of wind or water. The Alberici headquarters in Overland, Missouri, which won a LEED Platinum Award in 2004, uses solar panels to heat water and a 125-foot-tall wind turbine that provides the building with about 20 percent of its power. Wind currently provides only about 1 percent of America's electricity, but by 2020 that figure is expected to rise to 15 percent or higher. Some people believe that wind may be a major source of energy in the future.

Solar power is a more common source of power currently. Across America, solar panels placed on the roofs of buildings are helping to provide powers to homes, businesses, and even skyscrapers. Actor Brad Pitt has said that he believes people can live without depending on fossil fuels. "The idea that we pay utility bills is absolutely unnecessary,"[38] he says. Pitt is leading a project in New Orleans, Louisiana, helping to build ecohousing for people displaced by Hurricane Katrina in 2005. Pitt says that the energy-efficiency measures taken in building the homes will reduce upkeep costs by at least 75 percent.

Freedom Tower, which is being built on the former World Trade Center site in New York City, will also capitalize on renewable energy sources. Among the skyscraper's green features are massive solar panels and its own wind farm on the upper floors that are designed to meet much of the building's energy needs.

Solar panels and other ways to capture alternative energy are unlikely to completely replace fossil fuels in most buildings—at least in the near future. One obstacle is that they are expensive. Still, the costs are coming down as more and more people are buying them. "Most of these [energy-efficient] technologies are becoming off-the-shelf now, and increasingly affordable," says

Actor Brad Pitt talks about his home-building project in New Orleans in 2007.
The pink tents behind him represent where the eco-friendly houses will be built.

Ashok Gupta, the NRDC's chief energy economist. "It's just a matter of convincing consumers to demand the technologies and educating developers to continue integrating them in a holistic way."[39]

In addition to the expense, alternative energy has other drawbacks. Water has been used as a source of power for many years, but hydroelectric dams are expensive to build and maintain. They also require swiftly running water. Solar panels only work where—and when—the sun shines, and significant space is required to install the number of panels needed to provide energy for a large building. Similarly, wind power is generally not an option in mountainous or forested areas where the wind is blocked. Even in windy areas, such as the Great Plains, wind farms require a lot of physical space to produce electricity. Thus, in areas where land is at a premium, they are not a good option for providing energy.

Water Conservation

Green buildings go beyond traditional energy savings to look for ways to conserve water as well. Like other resources, water is a finite resource. Although 70 percent of the earth's surface is covered by water, less than 1 percent of this water is appropriate for human use.

In some buildings, gray water is used to flush toilets or water landscaping. Other buildings have systems—called catchment systems—that collect and treat rainwater to be used by the building.

Green homeowners can also fit their showers and faucets with fixtures designed to conserve water. The EPA mandates that showerheads use no more than 2.5 gallons of water per minute, and some water-saving showerheads that use much less water have become common. Toilets that flush a lot or a little water depending on how much is needed can conserve up to 80 percent of the annual water usage of a typical toilet.

Going for LEED

"People who in the past have had no environmental concern, because they want the LEED plaque and the marketing that goes along with that, they're thinking about these things." —Scott Horst, chair of the LEED steering committee.

Quoted in Daniel Brook, "It's Way Too Easy Being Green," *Slate*, December 26, 2007. www.slate.com/id/2180862/pagenum/2.

Some buildings have green roofs—literally. They have turf, plants, and sometimes even trees on their roofs. These green roofs help absorb rainwater and keep it from pouring off the building and washing soil away. In urban settings, they also create a bit of green space for birds, insects, and even people to enjoy.

If green roofs are an option, what about green walls? One of the designs submitted for Pitt's rebuilding projects in New Orleans includes ivy climbing up the walls. The ivy is a creative and green way to shade the homes and keep them cool in the Louisiana summer heat.

Landscaping

Landscaping involves how the yard around the building is designed and the kinds of plants and trees that are used. Using gravel driveways or stone pathways rather than paved surfaces is one way that landscapers are going green. Paved surfaces are impermeable, which means they do not allow water to seep back into the ground. Impermeable surfaces increase both the amount of water that runs into streets and gutters and the speed with which the water leaves the land. Runoff is not good for plants. It also picks up pesticides and fertilizers that are used to treat lawns and carries them into waterways. Some people believe that pesticides and fertilizers are responsible for 10 percent of the nation's water pollution.

Vegetation replaces tar and shingles on this Cincinnati, Ohio, rooftop. Green roofs help absorb rainwater and keep it from pouring off buildings and washing away soil.

Green advocates suggest cutting back on the amount of lawn used in landscaping, particularly if maintaining a beautiful grassy lawn requires a lot of chemicals and mowing. Covering the ground with ivy or planting more shrubs and trees is often a beautiful way to go green. The types of vegetation that are most "green" vary from one part of the country to another, but they are usually native to the area. Introducing plants from other areas can disturb the natural habitat of an area.

Although the greenest buildings address a multitude of factors, not all designers and builders of green homes start out with a comprehensive plan. "I bet there are plenty of people employing green technologies and techniques who may not even know it," says Ron Jones, the executive editor of *Green Building* magazine. "I'd bet just about any builder or manufacturer in this country is doing something for green building."[40]

CHAPTER 4

SHOPPING GREEN

Shelly White, a native of New York City, searches the stores in her small town in Pennsylvania for organic products. She has found a couple of stores that sell organic fruits and vegetables, but she says it is harder to find organic health and beauty products. Once a month, she heads to the mall to get products from the Body Shop, which only sells goods not tested on animals. She also looks for organic cottons and wools. Wherever she travels, White takes her own bags to tote her goods home. White is part of a growing number of consumers who are trying to help the environment by the shopping choices they make.

Going Organic

Organic foods are considered green because they do not add pesticides, fertilizers, or other pollutants to the land or waterways. Some people buy organic foods because they have less impact on the earth than other produce, but many people also believe that these foods taste better and are healthier for you.

To purchase organic food, people used to have to go to farm stands or farmers' markets where farmers bring their crops, or join a food cooperative that buys food from local organic farmers. Over the past couple of decades, however, supermarkets specializing in organic foods have sprung up in communities across America. Whole Foods is the biggest of these chains. As a growing number of consumers began to search out organic foods, major supermarket chains also began carrying organic produce and other natural foods.

Growing organic food requires more time and attention. Without artificial fertilizers, plants may not grow as big or yield as many fruits or vegetables. Without pesticides, some crops may be lost to bugs or other pests. In addition, organic foods are not treated with preservatives, so they may not be able to be transported as far or last as long. The lower yield—the amount that can be sold—means that the farmer will have to sell the produce at a higher price to make money. As a result, organic foods tend to cost more than other foods.

An increasing number of Americans are willing to pay higher prices for organics. In just one decade—from 1997 to 2006—sales of organic food grew by nearly 80 percent, to $17.7 billion. Kim Dennis, the mother of three young children, believes that the satisfaction of choosing a healthier alternative is worth the price. "I think it's definitely worth paying more," she says. "If [my children] eat a whole pint of berries, that's a lot of pesticides for their little bodies."[41]

Whole Foods is a supermarket chain specializing in organic foods.

Danger at Play

In the early 2000s, Americans were shocked to hear that their children's favorite toys might not be safe. Everything from Dora the Explorer dollhouses to Sesame Street bath toys were recalled after American companies learned that the plastic toys were made with lead, a substance that has been linked to health problems in children. Most of the plastic toys came from China.

The toy recall called attention to other items in our homes. People began to look again at the labels on their products and wonder what ingredients were used in making them.

Today's green consumers look for toys and other items made of wood or other natural materials rather than plastic. They avoid toys that have glues or paints with VOCs. In addition, they avoid a plastic called polyvinyl chloride (PVC), which is often found in beach toys, dolls, and other soft plastic toys. Green consumers say that PVC releases dangerous toxins into the environment.

Some green consumers also look for products made close to home. They point out it takes a lot of fuel to ship products from faraway places. "Cutting down the length a toy has traveled to your front door is a greener option," writes author Sean Fisher. "As a bonus, locally made toys are often hand-made and unique."

Sean Fisher, "How to Green Your Kids' Toys," TreeHugger, May 26, 2007. www.treehugger.com/files/2007/05/how-to-green-your-kids-toys.php.

Closely related to the organic movement is the desire for fruits, vegetables, and other foods that are grown locally. Green consumers believe that buying local foods is better for the environment. Food that is grown nearby is generally fresher because it gets to the store or farm stand faster. Buying locally also means that food is not transported great distances, decreasing fuel consumption and air pollution.

Health and Beauty Products

When she shops for health and beauty products, Flavia Kawaja, an interior designer who lives in New York City, reads the labels carefully. She will not buy antiperspirants with aluminum or products containing parabens, which are often used as preservatives in soaps and shampoos. She also avoids products with dyes. Kawaja is part of the growing number of green consumers who believe that what you put on your body is as important to your health as what you put in your body.

These consumers are fueling a growing demand for organic health and beauty products. According to the Organic Trade Association, Americans spent $350 million on organic personal products in 2006. This is $68 million more than in 2005. Companies that market natural products, such as Burt's Bees, Jason Natural Cosmetics, and Tom's of Maine, are all experiencing rapid growth in sales. Several organic companies, including Origins and Nature's Gate, have received certification for some of their products from the U.S. Department of Agriculture proving that their products contain organic ingredients.

Natural soaps are made without chemicals or artificial ingredients. Many people now believe that what you put on your body is as important to your health as what you put in your body.

Experts caution that natural products may not always be as healthy as people assume, however. "Consumers should not necessarily assume that an 'organic' or 'natural' ingredient or product would possess greater inherent safety than another chemically identical version of the same ingredient," says Linda M. Katz, the director of the Food and Drug Administration's Office of Cosmetics and Colors. "In fact, 'natural' ingredients may be harder to preserve against microbial contamination and growth than synthetic raw materials."[42]

Jane Houlihan, the vice president for research of the non-profit Environmental Working Group, Washington, D.C., concurs. In their effort to attract green consumers, Houlihan says, some companies are using new natural products that have not been adequately tested for safety. "Just because an ingredient comes from a plant does not necessarily make it safe to use in a cosmetic," Houlihan explains. "Tobacco, hemlock and poison ivy are all examples of plants that can be hazardous."[43]

Organic Clothing and Fabrics

Although people are most familiar with organic foods, truly green consumers scrutinize the labels of other products looking for natural fibers and materials. Clothing, sheets, and upholstery for chairs and sofas—all these fabrics can be made from cotton, wool, silk, or hemp that have not been treated with chemicals or pesticides. In addition to being better for the environment, some people think organic fabrics are softer and feel better against the skin.

Patagonia was considered a pioneer when it switched to organic cotton in 1996. "Going organic was a difficult decision for us," says a spokesperson for the company. "Ethically it made perfect sense, but it was expensive and hard to come by. Today, thanks to our friends and customers, we're still selling organic cotton clothing, and more and more businesses are making the switch because you voted with your dollars."[44]

As the number of green consumers swells, more companies are adding clothes made exclusively of organic cotton to their lines. For instance, Levi Strauss launched a line of all-organic "eco" jeans in 2006. In 2007, the Gap introduced a line of organic cotton T-shirts for men that are unbleached and made without any chemical dyes. Although clothing made from organic fabrics tends to cost more, green consumers hope that as more companies offer organics, the cost will come down.

The Green Clean

EPA studies show that indoor air is much more polluted than the air we breathe outside. In some places, the air we breathe indoors is five times worse than outdoors. One of the reasons is that the paints and glues in many traditional building materials include volatile organic compounds (VOCs), chemicals that produce toxic fumes. These chemicals, released in a process called off-gassing, can make people sick.

Healthier, greener products avoid the use of VOCs. "When you're making furniture, you don't want toxic dust coming off of the materials that you are cutting," says Sam Kragiel, a designer with Brave Space Design. "You don't want to use finishes that are hazardous for yourself and the consumer and for the environment as a whole. That's what has led us toward using environmentally sustainable materials."[45]

SHOPPING RESPONSIBLY

"I love to shop, I love to cook, I love to feel that I have done one thing a day to educate myself and my children in making the world a better, stronger place to live in. Easier said than done, right? We would all do the right thing/things if only we had the resources, the answers, the advice we need." —Julia Roberts, award-winning actress and environmentalist.

Julia Roberts, foreword to *Gorgeously Green: 8 Simple Steps to an Eco-Friendly Life*, by Sophie Uliano. New York: HarperCollins, 2008, p. x.

Low-VOC and zero-VOC products are becoming standard options in the marketplace. Major paint companies such as Benjamin Moore and Olympic now offer low-VOC or zero-VOC paints. Lowe's and Home Depot also offer lines of eco-friendly paints. Other companies have jumped on the green

Indoor air can be toxic to breathe if the wrong chemicals are used. As a result, many people are using "eco-cleaners," which do not give off fumes because they do not include hazardous ingredients.

bandwagon by offering natural alternatives to paint, such as clay-based plaster.

Paint and other finishes are not the only toxins often found at home. The EPA estimates that from three to twenty-five gallons of toxic materials are present in the average U.S. household, most of which are in cleaning materials. Bleaches, ammonias, and other chemicals used to clean bathrooms, floors, and countertops are among the toxic products many of us have in our homes.

Green consumers can clean their homes with natural ingredients like water, vinegar, baking soda—and a lot of elbow grease. Fortunately for green consumers, however, there are a number of "eco-cleaners" on the market that work as well as conventional cleaning fluids. Because they do not have hazardous ingredients, they do not give off fumes when used. When emptied into the sink or toilet, they will not pollute the water, either.

A Plethora of Plastic

The amount of plastic packaging used to display and ship goods is staggering. Some people say that plastic is our greatest garbage challenge. According to the EPA, packaging amounts to more than one-third of the municipal solid waste by weight. Americans use about 32 billion pounds of plastic each year. Used for everything from toys to automobile parts to food containers, plastics never biodegrade—they remain with us always. Over hundreds of years, plastic may break down into smaller particles, but it releases toxic gases in the process. In addition to the energy needed to dispose of or recycle the plastic after it is used, it takes a great deal of energy to make the plastic in the first place.

ORGANICS: NOT BETTER, NOT WORSE

"Organic agriculture is just another method of agriculture—not better, not worse. This is like any other merchandising scheme we have, which is providing customers what they want. For those customers looking for an organic alternative in things like Rice Krispies, we now have an alternative for them." —Bruce Peterson, head of perishable food at Wal-Mart, which recently introduced a line of organic foods.

Melanie Warner, "Wal-Mart Eyes Organic Foods," *New York Times,* May 12, 2006. www
.nytimes.com/2006/05/12/business/12organic.html?_r=1&scp=1&sq=wal-mart%20
eyes%20organic%20foods&st=cse&oref=slogin.

Green manufacturers and designers are searching for solutions through groups such as the Sustainable Packaging Coalition. Some green consumers are just saying no. Green consumers look for opportunities to reduce their dependence on these plastic bags. They buy loose fruits and vegetables, putting them right into the grocery cart rather than the plastic bags supermarkets provide to tote them. They also look for nuts, beans, and other goods that can be bought in bulk, without plastic packaging. Some green consumers have taken things one step further by baking their own bread and even making cheese to avoid buying things wrapped in plastic.

SHOPPING AS POLITICS

"What I hear as I talk to people is this phenomenal sense of despair about their inability to do anything about climate change, or the disparity between rich and poor. But when they go into a grocery store they can do something—they can make decisions about what they are buying and send a very clear message." —Marion Nestle, a nutritionist at New York University and the author of *Food Politics*.

Quoted in *Economist*, "Food Politics," December 7, 2006. www.economist.com/business/displaystory.cfm?story_id=8380592.

Beth Terry, a blogger who tracks her weekly consumption of plastic on her Web site, sends back packaging to online retailers, with a letter urging the company to reconsider their use—or overuse—of packaging. "In my efforts to tread lightly on the earth, I am seeking to reduce the amount of waste I produce considerably," she writes. "I find extra packaging of this kind to be unnecessary, and . . . they are plastic, which is not biodegradable and will last in the environment forever, whether it is recycled or not. I urge you to rethink the amount of packaging used to ship DVDs in the future."[46]

Still, it appears that packaging is here to stay. In a 2002 survey by *Packaging World* magazine, only 30 percent of respondents—who made food, personal care, and pharmaceutical products for consumers—said that environmentally friendly packaging was "very important." When asked if consumers would pay a premium for green packaging, 61 percent said no.

Plastic or Paper?

Another concern is the thin plastic bags provided at supermarket checkout stands. According to Planet Ark, Americans use

100 billion of these bags per year—an average of 552 per family. Worldwide, more than two hundred thousand plastic bags are thrown into landfills every hour. Most of these bags are used just once—and for a very short time—to cart groceries home from the store. There is so little plastic in these lightweight bags that recycling is simply not practical—it takes too much energy to melt down the plastic to make it worth the effort. Like all plastic, the bags will never biodegrade.

America generates about 32 billion pounds of plastic each year. Plastic stays around forever because it never biodegrades, which creates a huge environmental concern.

These Eco Easy shopping bags are made from recycled materials and are a green alternative to plastic bags.

Actor and environmentalist Edward Norton has the following advice: "People say, 'What's the one thing they could do to help?' I say you gotta do more than one thing, [but] one thing for sure is the bags. Plastic bags are turning out to be one of the worst things we're doing to the environment. That is a simple, small thing that everybody can do—forget about those silly plastic bags."[47]

Ireland sought to deal with the plastic bags by levying a tax on them. The tax raised millions of dollars that were then spent on environmental programs. The tax also reduced consumption of the bags by 90 percent. Cities in the United States are also looking at taxing or outlawing the bags. In March 2008, San Francisco became the first U.S. city to outlaw the use of plastic grocery bags. Supermarkets and pharmacies are required to use compostable bags made of cornstarch or bags made of recyclable paper.

Not everyone believes that the plastic bags should be banned, however. The bags serve an important purpose. They help keep food from spoiling. They also say there is very little plastic in these bags, making them better than other options.

Some people think paper bags are better than plastic because they are easier to reuse and are biodegradable. But paper bags also have disadvantages. Paper bags are thicker than plastic bags, so they cost more to transport. In addition, they are made from trees. Millions of trees are cut down to make paper bags, causing forests to be lost. And like plastic bags, most paper bags

Buying and Selling Used on the Internet

The rise of the Internet has opened a number of new doors for finding "gently used" items. When Nick Clark wants to buy something for one of his sons—a foosball table or lacrosse stick—he searches Craigslist for a bargain. "You have to spend time looking," says Clark, "but there are some great deals out there."

The Clarks are part of a growing trend in America. Millions of Americans buy and sell goods on eBay, Craigslist, and other Internet sites each month. Some people also use sites like Freecycle to give away items they no longer want. This is a green option because it extends the life of an item and keeps it from heading to the landfill before its time. In addition, sharing resources in this way means that fewer new items need to be made, saving energy and raw materials.

Nick Clark, personal interview, July 10, 2008.

end up in landfills after just one use. Paper does not degrade in landfills as well as most people think.

Is Organic Food as Green as It Seems?

"You cannot say that all organic food is better for the environment than all food grown conventionally. If you look carefully at the amount of energy required to produce these foods you get a complicated picture. In some cases, the carbon footprint for organics is larger." —Ken Green, professor of environmental management at Manchester Business School, England.

Quoted in Cahal Milmo, "Organic Farming 'No Better for the Environment,'" *Independent*, February 19, 2007. www.independent.co.uk/environment/green-living/organic-farming-no-better-for-the-environment-436949.html.

The greenest solution is to bring reusable bags to the supermarket. Some stores sell bags made specifically for carrying groceries or other goods. Many of these bags are made of sturdy plastic, but an increasing number are made from earth-friendly materials such as hemp or linen. Some supermarket chains also offer a few cents back for each reusable bag of groceries they fill. Supermarkets do this not only to enhance their green image; it also saves them the expense of all those plastic and paper bags!

Reducing Bottles, Cans, and Other Packaging

Bottled water is emerging as another hot topic. A 2007 article by Charles Fishman in *Fast Company* magazine reports that North Americans spent $15 billion on bottled water in 2006. The process of making plastic requires oil; Fishman says that making plastic bottles uses the same amount of oil as one hundred thousand cars each year. Most of these bottles—85 to 90 percent of them—are thrown out, mostly because we tend to use them when we are on the go.

Talk-show host Ellen DeGeneres counts not recycling plastic water bottles among her pet peeves: "I've seen people drinking water out of plastic bottles and then not recycling them. That's infuriating. I know it's faster to throw it in the garbage.

But if you're going to buy water individually bottled for your convenience, then all I say is, take the time and put it in the can marked 'Recycle.' It's a small thing that makes a big difference."[48]

Really green consumers say that it does not make enough of a difference to recycle these bottles. They say that we should not use the bottles in the first place. Not only is energy lost in bottling water, they say, but it also wastes water. Buying a filter for the kitchen tap and filling a heavy-duty reusable bottle with tap water is a far greener strategy.

In fact, this strategy can be extended to any individually packaged item. Rather than purchasing juice boxes for school lunches, green consumers buy a large container of juice and pour it into a Thermos. The same goes for individually packaged snack

In an effort to cut down on the plastic that bottled water generates, many restaurants are serving their own filtered tap water as an alternative.

foods: Buying crackers, cookies, and chips in large packages and putting them into reusable containers for school can reduce waste considerably.

Of course, all packaging is not bad, even if it is not recyclable. Some packaging protects goods and keeps them from getting broken or damaged during transport. In this way, packaging reduces waste. Packaging may also maximize the amount of a product that can be packed into a larger container. As a result, fewer containers—and thus fewer trucks—may be needed to move the same amount of goods. This means lower greenhouse gas emissions in the end.

Buying Used and Recycled Products

Another option for green shoppers is buying items that have been used by someone else. Sometimes people sell things after only one use. When people buy used computer games, videos, Legos, building blocks, or books, they are saving the raw materials and energy needed to make new ones.

Green consumers also look for products with recycled content. Napkins, toilet tissue, or printer paper can be made from paper that has already been used. The recycled content can be as little as 5 percent or as much as 100 percent.

Many green consumers say recycled products are just as good as new. One reporter set out to compare paper products made with recycled content to those made with new paper. While his family was away, he replaced his household's paper products with recycled brands. "After three days and zero comments, I took that as a sign that we could live happily ever after with recycled,"[49] he reports.

Products made with recycled ingredients can be hard to find. For example, none of the best-selling brands of napkins, paper towels, tissues, or toilet paper has any recycled content. "Where I live I have to really look for recycled items," writes a frustrated consumer. "They're not readily available and often cost more when I do find them. There's not much choice either: toilet paper, paper towels, tissues and some office supplies."[50]

It used to be difficult to find green products, but an increasing number of companies recognize that going green is good for

A truck loaded with recycled paper leaves a paper mill in California. Many people cannot tell the difference between items made with recycled paper and new paper.

business. In an effort to attract green consumers, retailers are adding products made from organic, recycled, and recyclable materials. Wal-Mart—a chain known for offering a wide range of products at low prices—introduced a line of organic products in 2006. With more retailers offering more options, green products are not only becoming easier to find, they are becoming less expensive as well. Many people have shown they are willing to pay more for products that are better for the environment. Many more will likely go green as costs become more competitive.

CHAPTER 5

REDUCE, REUSE, RECYCLE

According to the EPA, in 2006, U.S. residents, businesses, and institutions produced more than 251 million tons of waste—about 4.6 pounds per person per day. The amount of trash the average American throws out is at least twice as much as the average person in western Europe. But the garbage represents a far greater problem. In their book *Cradle to Cradle*, William McDonough and Michael Braungart write, "What most people see in their garbage cans is just the tip of a material iceberg: the product itself contains on average only 5 percent of the raw materials involved in the process of making and delivering it."[51]

Most of this trash is disposed of in landfills. Landfills are simply large pits where garbage is buried. Most of the landfills in the United States are far from where people live. Unlike the landfills of old, today's U.S. landfills are relatively clean and well managed.

Unfortunately, some of our trash never makes it to a landfill. It blows out of garbage cans into city streets and waterways. In a 2006 special report on the state of our oceans and waterways, the *Los Angeles Times* reported that a pile of trash twice the size of Texas floats in the Pacific Ocean. Some of the garbage washes up on distant shores or is eaten by seabirds that mistake it for food. Scientists say plastic, which birds cannot digest, kills thousands of birds each year. "Unfortunately, over time, plastics will become more and more prevalent in our oceans," says John Klavitter, a wildlife biologist with the U.S. Fish and Wildlife Service at Midway Atoll. "I hate to become pessimistic, but the problem will probably become worse before it becomes better."[52]

To combat this problem, educators emphasize the "three Rs" of going green—reduce, reuse, and recycle. Reducing begins with the consumer. In addition to conserving energy and water, reducing includes thinking about the choices you make when shopping. Avoiding packaging, buying used products, and buying only what you need are the main strategies for reducing waste. Some people have gone green by avoiding all paper products, for instance. They use cloth napkins and towels rather than paper products. They never buy paper or plastic plates or cups. They also prefer cloth diapers over disposables. In general, they look for products that will not be thrown out after just one use.

Finding New Uses for Old Stuff

Reusing materials involves making them last longer than their "natural" shelf life. An old shirt might be used as a rag to dust the furniture, for example, or a used toothbrush might be used to clean the grout in the bathroom. Sometimes reuse involves a bit of creativity, as when used corks from wine bottles are crafted into a bulletin board.

Discarded plastic is a constant hazard to animals in the wild. Here, a mallard has become tangled in a plastic ring.

Giving It Away to Charity

Rather than throwing out things they no longer want, green consumers look for places to make donations. Some charity organizations have special drop-off centers; others pick up items from a person's home, making going green easier than ever.

Habitat for Humanity, a nonprofit organization that helps to build homes for needy people, accepts tools, building materials, furniture, and appliances in good working order. Habitat for Humanity either uses these items in their projects or sells them to help raise funds. The Salvation Army, Goodwill Industries, and Purple Heart operate local centers that accept household and clothing items for resale. They also often pick up donated items.

Specialty stores often accept specific donations. Office Depot and Staples, for instance, accept toner cartridges and some other types of office supplies. Eyeglass stores often collect eyeglasses for the needy. Local charity organizations, hospitals, libraries, schools, daycare centers, homeless shelters, and churches are also often in need of household goods, clothing, books, and even those little Happy Meal toys from McDonald's!

By using objects intended for the trash—and avoiding the need to buy other items to accomplish these purposes—reuse helps people tread more lightly on the environment. Reuse usually extends the life of an item for a limited amount of time, however. The rag and toothbrush are likely to end up in a landfill after they have served their cleaning purposes.

Recycling

Recycling materials is different from reusing them. Recycling converts old products into new ones by mechanical or chemical methods. Used steel or aluminum cans, for instance, are shredded, melted, and then reformed to make new cans or other products.

In many communities, recyclable materials are picked up as part of their waste collection services. Where this is not an option, people may drive used glass, plastics, newspapers, or other recyclables to collection centers that are managed by the local government, an environmental group, or a business. Several different kinds of businesses handle recyclable materials after they are collected. One of the main challenges for recycling programs is converting the used paper, glass, metal, and plastic into a useful product and finding people and businesses that are willing to buy these new products.

Many people believe that recycling programs should be in place throughout the United States. Representative Edward Markey introduced legislation that would require all Americans to pay a deposit on glass and plastic bottles and on aluminum cans.

Individuals play a critical role in waste reduction and recycling. Education programs abound to help people understand the benefits of recycling, what can be recycled, and how recyclables should be sorted. Many governments also offer incentives to encourage recycling. Currently, eleven states have programs that charge consumers a deposit on their beverage cans and bottles. To get back the deposit—usually 5 or 10 cents per container—consumers must return the cans or bottles. Recycling rates are twice as high in states with such bottle bills than in those without them.

Some leaders believe these state recycling programs should be applied throughout the United States. In the fall of 2007, Representative Edward Markey of Massachusetts introduced legislation that would require all Americans to pay a deposit on glass and plastic bottles and on aluminum cans. Markey says, "Recycling is an everyday action that we can all take to cut global warming emissions and be good environmental stewards. Our national goal should be to one day recycle every single bottle we use."[53]

IS WASTE MANAGEMENT AN URGENT PROBLEM?

"I find it hard to argue that waste management is our most urgent environmental problem. At most, it is one among many issues that clamor for our attention. Other problems pose more serious threats to our well-being than the disposal of solid waste."
—Frank Ackerman, a solid waste expert.

Quoted in Michael Brower and Warren Leon, *The Consumer's Guide to Effective Environmental Choices: Practical Advice from the Union of Concerned Scientists.* New York: Three Rivers Press, 1999, pp. 38–39.

Paper

According to Carnegie Mellon University's recycling Web site, American businesses generate enough paper each day to circle the globe at least 40 times. The typical business office generates about 1.5 pounds of wastepaper per employee each day. Seventy-seven percent of this paper is recyclable.

Paper recycling is standard in many—if not most—schools and businesses. In addition, household recycling programs often

A driver works on his truck at a Waste Management processing facility in Illinois. Waste Management recycles over 1 million tons of glass each year.

include newspapers, magazines, and cardboard. Waste Management, one of the nation's largest trash companies, recycles more than 1 million tons of glass each year. Eighty percent of the glass that is recycled is made into new glass bottles.

The process of making new paper from old is relatively simple. Recycling paper uses just half of the energy required to make paper from trees. "Virgin papermaking is one of the most environmentally harmful industries on earth," writes Elizabeth Royte in *Garbage Land*. "It depletes the forests and their biodiversity, it uses more water than any other industrial process in the nation, . . . and it dumps billions of gallons of water contaminated with chlorinated dioxin and a host of other hazardous and conventional pollutants into rivers, lakes, and harbors."[54]

One of the difficulties in paper recycling is that prices fluctuate widely. In 1993, the average selling price of recycled paper was $46 per ton; just two years later, the price had escalated to $165 per ton. In the first decade of the twenty-first century, the price is back to $50 per ton. Because buyers cannot know how much they will have to pay for recycled materials from one year to the next, such drastic price changes make it difficult for buyers to be able to plan. This forced some early recycling programs to shut down.

Still, Allen Hershkowitz of the NRDC emphasizes the importance of recycling paper at any cost. "We've got to keep doing it, even if we're just holding the line," he says. "Conservatively, timber harvests would expand fifty percent in the next thirty-five years if we didn't recycle paper."[55]

Metal, Glass, and Plastic Containers

Regardless of the metal, mining is harmful to the environment. Digging into the land damages habitats, destroys natural resources, and produces carbon dioxide and acid rain. Finding and extracting metals also requires a substantial amount of energy.

RECYCLING IS EASY

"You don't have to change the way you live to recycle. It really isn't all that big of a commitment. It's more about just being conscious of your waste. When you can see the difference recycling makes in your house, you can begin to imagine how big an impact it can have on the world." —Faith Hill and Tim McGraw, married country music stars who have written about their concerns for the environment.

Quoted in Elizabeth Rogers and Thomas M. Kostigen, *The Green Book: The Everyday Guide to Saving the Planet One Simple Step at a Time.* New York: Three Rivers Press, 2007, p. 51.

Fortunately, metals are relatively easy and cost effective to recycle. Working with clean recycled steel instead of forging new steel from raw materials also cuts air pollution by more than 85 percent and water usage by 40 percent. Recycling steel also conserves enough energy annually to power about 18 million homes for twelve months. According to the Steel Recycling Institute, 70 million tons of steel scrap is recycled each year— enough steel to build 189 professional football stadiums.

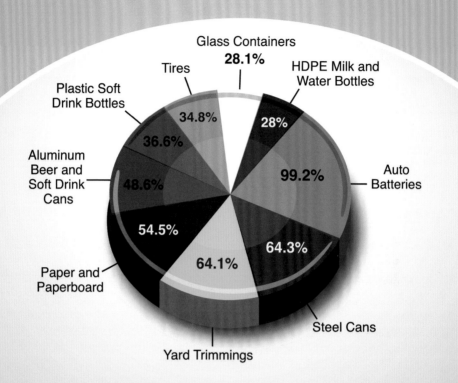

Recycling Rates, 2007

Glass Containers
28.1%

Tires

HDPE Milk and Water Bottles

Plastic Soft Drink Bottles

34.8%

28%

36.6%

Aluminum Beer and Soft Drink Cans

48.6%

99.2%

Auto Batteries

54.5%

Paper and Paperboard

64.1%

64.3%

Yard Trimmings

Steel Cans

Taken from: www.epa.gov/osw/facts-text.htm.

American households do their part by recycling steel cans. With a rate of 62.9 percent, steel cans are among the most widely recycled household items. Americans also use—and recycle—a lot of aluminum cans. The Worldwatch Institute says that Americans drink the contents of 100 billion aluminum cans per year—amounting to half of the total number used worldwide. Roughly 45 percent of these cans are recycled. Recycling aluminum takes less than 10 percent of the energy needed to make new aluminum. In fact, recycling just one can saves enough energy to power a computer for ten hours.

Like paper, glass is relatively easy to recycle. After glass jars and bottles are electronically sorted according to color, they are usually ground down by machines and then made into new bottles. Recycling glass requires less energy than recycling plastic or aluminum. It also saves as much as 70 percent in raw materials.

A Little Effort Can Make a Big Difference

We can all go a little more green. Here are just a few of the things you can do:

- Walk or bike to where you need to go.
- Carpool to school events and parties, or offer a neighbor a ride.
- Take shorter showers. Turn off the water when not in use.
- Use rechargeable batteries in your games and other gadgets.
- Use less electricity by turning off the television, radio, and lights when you are not in the room. Unplug your clock radio and appliances when you go on vacation.

- Use a lunchbox, Thermos, and reusable containers. Avoid plastic baggies and individually packaged items.
- Look for ways to make things last longer. Use both sides of paper when printing things on the computer, for instance. Give away things you are no longer using.
- Recycle newspapers, glass, plastic bottles, and aluminum cans. Rinse them out and sort them according to the requirements of the collection agency.
- Buy products made from recycled materials.
- Start a composting pile.

Yet, despite the ease of recycling glass, only about 25 percent of the glass we use is recycled. In addition, glass containers are increasingly being replaced with plastics, which are far more harmful to the environment.

Plastic can also be recycled. Because there are so many different kinds of plastics, however, used containers first must be sorted by type. In most cases, the type of plastic used for a container is identified with a numbered triangle symbol on the bottom. Most municipal recycling programs accept only some kinds of plastics.

Recycling plastic involves crushing the sorted containers into small pieces that are melted or treated with chemicals. The resulting liquid plastic is then formed into new products. In addition to new plastic containers or parts, recycled plastic is sometimes woven into fiber that is used to make carpets or clothing. Fleece is one of the most common fabrics made from plastic. Manufacturers also re-form used plastic into attractive outdoor furniture, decks, and docks, replacing the wood once used for these purposes. The plastic goods cost more than wood, but consumers say they are worth the extra cost. Because they will not wear away due to water or be eaten by bugs, the decks and docks will last much longer in the great outdoors.

To Market

For any product, the last step of the recycling process is selling the new product. Unfortunately, it can be hard to find markets for some types of recyclables. Plastic companies generally prefer new plastic, for instance, because it is of more consistent quality than recycled plastic. The new plastic is guaranteed to be free of incompatible polymers—the chemical from which plastics are made—that sometimes are mixed in when the plastic is not sorted well before recycling. Manufacturers say it is also easier to control the color of plastics that have no recycled content. Similarly, paper manufacturers complain that recycled paper often gets dirty during collection and sorting. The added expense of cleaning the paper makes it too expensive to use for some purposes.

Our Throw-Away Society

"We live in a throw-away society. You'd be amazed at what some people throw away—everything from bathtubs to books. But the truth is, there's no such place as 'away.'" —David Bach.

David Bach, with Hillary Rosner, *Go Green, Live Rich: 50 Simple Ways to Save the Earth and Get Rich Trying.* New York: Broadway Books, 2008, p. 88.

Some companies believe that putting "recycled" on the label will make people think that it is of poor quality. "Consumers have long been trained to think of previously used stuff as inferior," explains Richard C. Porter, an economist and author of *The Economics of Waste.* "This training goes back centuries, to the time when recycled clothing made of recycled rags was called 'shoddy,' and the very word 'recycled' became a synonym for second rate."[56]

Is Recycling the Answer?

Some people say that recycling is a waste of time and money. At a public hearing in March 2006, Tom Phillips, an elected official in Greensboro, North Carolina, said, "The net cost for recycling is more than double the cost for regular garbage collection that will go to the transfer station. (This is after selling the recyclables we can.) A lot of what we recycle winds up at the landfill anyway because of contamination or lack of markets for the recycled material. . . . While [recycling] 'feels good' it is too expensive and we must look for better alternatives."[57]

Some economists argue that recycling will occur naturally when there is a market for recyclables, as with large pieces of scrap steel and aluminum. Michael Munger, a political science professor at Duke University, believes that recycling makes no sense for other items. "There is a simple test for determining whether something is a resource or just garbage," Munger writes.

Workers sort through cardboard, plastic, and paper at a recycling plant in Newark, New Jersey, in 2008. Some people feel that while recycling feels good, it is also too expensive, and other alternative methods of waste management must be explored.

"If someone will pay you for the item, it's a resource. . . . But if you have to pay someone to take the item away . . . then the item is garbage."[58]

In some cases, the process of recycling some products creates more pollution than it is worth. Recycling simply may not be the answer for many materials. Ann Leonard, an expert in international sustainability and environmental health issues, explains: "True closed-loop recycling has no new resource input and no waste output. And that's virtually impossible with plastic waste because its chemical structure changes when it's heated and the quality degrades. We're just delaying its eventual dumping."[59]

TODAY'S LANDFILL

"Recycling does sometimes make sense—for some materials in some places at some times. But the simplest and cheapest option is usually to bury garbage in an environmentally safe landfill. And since there's no shortage of landfill space . . . , there's no reason to make recycling a legal or moral imperative." —John Tierney.

John Tierney, "Recycling Is Garbage," *New York Times*, June 30, 1996. http://query.nytimes.com/gst/fullpage.html?res=990CE1DF1339F933A05755C0A960958260.

Composting

Although composting is usually ignored by many recycling programs, it is a type of recycling. In fact, composting can be a very effective way to recycle food scraps, yard waste, and other organic materials and keep them out of landfills.

The U.S. Environmental Protection Agency indicates that 24 percent of the U.S. waste stream is made up of yard trimmings and food scraps. Composting is a system whereby these organic materials are combined, aerated, and made into a rich mulch.

The Internet teems with information for families who are interested in starting a compost pile, and a number of products—such as bins to house the compost and boxes to help aerate it—are readily available. Usually, composting consists primarily of separating out fruit and vegetable peels, coffee grounds, yard waste,

A Whole Foods Market employee disposes of pineapple ends that will be emptied into a compost bin to be recycled. Composting is a very effective way of recycling.

and other organic materials and putting them in a backyard compost bin or heap. Nature does the rest of the work.

Some companies and schools also compost the waste from their cafeterias. Brentwood Elementary School in Brentwood, Texas, for instance, collects fifteen to twenty pounds of raw fruits and vegetables from the cafeteria each day to add to its compost pile. The school's gardening and environmental clubs maintain the compost piles and use the finished compost in the school gardens.

In West Warwick, Rhode Island, Cox Communications became the first large company in the state to add food scraps from its cafeteria to the list of items it recycles. "Anything we can do to reduce the stuff we send [to the state Central Landfill] and send it to a place where it adds some value is a good thing for the community,"[60] explains Brad Shipp, Cox's vice president of information technology. "I believe more companies will look into composting because it is so good for the environment," says Alyson Silva, the commercial recycling coordinator in Rhode Island's Office of Waste Management. "Organics are a big part of the waste stream for businesses such as hotels, restaurants and bars."[61]

Not everyone has a yard where they can compost their organic waste. One option for apartment dwellers is to worm compost, or vermicompost. This type of composting is increasing in popularity among green advocates in urban areas. "I discovered that a couple of pounds of wriggling worms can turn my kitchen scraps into nutrient-rich compost in about 60 days," writes Joan D. Filsinger, an avid gardener who explains how the process works. "There's little or no odor, and no heavy lifting. And, best of all, my worms make compost in a compact container right in my own home."[62]

Alixe Dancer took a course on worm composting offered by Bronx Green-Up, an organization in New York that helps educate people about green practices. Dancer and her mother keep a worm bin in their Bronx apartment. Bread, grains, coffee grounds and filters, teabags, eggshells, and fruit and vegetable scraps are all decomposed by the wiggly worms. "It's an ecosystem all in itself,"[63] Dancer says. According to Jodie Colón, the compost educator for Bronx Green-Up, interest in workshops on worm composting is increasing exponentially. "People are looking for things they can do," she explains. "This type of composting is really accessible."[64]

Compost Collection

For those who do not want worms in their apartments, local governments have begun to establish central composting sites. Most often, these composting sites are used primarily for yard waste, but some also allow some types of food scraps to be included. In many cases, after the material has been composted, the city gives or sells the compost back to citizens, who use it in their yards or gardens. In this way, government composting programs provide two services: They keep organic waste out of landfills, and they provide compost material at reasonable prices.

In Rapid City, South Dakota, city administrators launched a small-scale composting program in 1993. Since then, the recycling of yard waste has grown to approximately four thousand tons per year. Rapid City combines the yard waste with biosolids, or sludge, from its municipal waste program to create compost. The resulting compost is used for municipal projects and sold to area residents.

Not surprisingly, the number of municipalities that provide composting services for residents has increased exponentially. Across the nation, the number of municipal composting sites rose from 651 in 1989 to 3,227 in 2002. State governments have also passed laws designed to reduce the amount of yard waste. Thirty-five states recycle yard trimmings, food scraps, and/or wood, and twenty-one states have banned these materials from landfills.

Worm composting is popular among green apartment dwellers. Also, in 2006, the state of California encouraged employees to bring worms to work. The worms would chew up food scraps to produce compost, which employees could then take home to use as an all-natural fertilizer.

Is Compost All Green?

American cities have come a long way since the 1990s, when more than 90 percent of organic waste was disposed of in landfills. In 2006, 62 percent of the 32 million tons of yard trimmings was composted or otherwise recycled—by making wood chips of tree branches, for example. Just 2.6 percent of food waste was included in this compost, however.

Like most green practices, composting has its critics. Tom Outerbridge, who works with a nonprofit called City Green in New York City, says, "People think composting is the greatest system in the world. But it takes a lot of energy to make it work—to deal with odor abatement and collecting it and turning it to aerate it."[65] Outerbridge says that four trucks once circled some New York City neighborhoods: one collecting garbage; another collecting metal, plastic, and glass; another collecting paper; and yet another for compost. "Those trucks have a huge environmental impact," he says. "And then there are all the trucks and bulldozers pushing the compost around at the facility."[66]

There are also other expenses involved in composting on a large scale. Most yard waste is collected in the summer and fall, then made into mulch, which is then sold in the spring. Space is needed to store it, which can be expensive in urban areas. It can also be difficult to find buyers.

Still, advocates point out that composting is about much more than the compost. "In spite of the obvious benefit, producing a saleable, organic product may not be the most significant payoff of municipal composting in the long run," writes James I. Miller in *American Recycler*. "In conjunction with curbside or community recycling efforts, successful programs involving composting are becoming an important and beneficial tool for diverting solid organic waste from our nation's landfills."[67] Rapid City's composting system is expected to extend the lifetime of its municipal landfill by more than thirty years.

Into the Future

Anthropologist Margaret Mead once said, "We won't have a society if we destroy the environment." She also said that it was not enough to leave it up to someone else to take care of the

Compost sludge is loaded into a truck in Fairbanks, Alaska. It can often be difficult to find buyers for compost, but this compost regularly sells out because they cannot make enough to meet the demand from local gardeners and landscapers.

environment. "Never doubt that a small group of thoughtful, committed citizens can change the world. Indeed, it is the only thing that ever has."[68]

Still, with so many ways to go green, it can be difficult for the average consumer to know where to start. Advocates of going green know it can be confusing. They suggest starting simply. Turning off a light switch, unplugging a cell phone, or walking a half mile to the library seem like small steps, but they soon become habits. If everyone adopts just a few green habits, the earth will benefit.

In her book *Gorgeously Green*, Sophie Uliano describes this approach: "If I make one tiny positive change today, I consider myself green. It can be as simple as flicking off a light switch or buying an organic apple. My motto is one change makes a difference, and if you can make two, that's even better!"[69]

Uliano is right: Every little bit counts. By taking small actions, each person can help to make the world a healthier place.

Chapter 1: Why Green?

1. TreeHugger, "How to Go Green," www.treehugger.com/go green.php.

2. Gary Levin, "Planet Green TV Network Pushes Environmentalism," *USA Today*, March 31, 2008. www.usatoday.com/life/television/news/2008-03-30-planet-green_N.htm.

3. Quoted in Levin, "Planet Green TV Network Pushes Environmentalism."

4. Quoted in Roger Ebert, "An Inconvenient Truth," *Chicago Sun-Times,* June 2, 2006. http://rogerebert.suntimes.com/apps/pbcs .dll/article?AID=/20060601/REVIEWS/60517002/1023.

5. Ebert, "An Inconvenient Truth."

6. Quoted in Confederate Yankee, "An Inconvenient Truth for Al Gore," March 13, 2007. http://confederateyankee.mu.nu/archives/218760.php.

7. Quoted in Natasha Singer, "Natural, Organic Beauty," *New York Times*, November 1, 2007. www.nytimes.com/2007/11/01/fashion/01skin.html.

8. Quoted in Jesse Ellison, "Save the Planet, Lose the Guilt," *Newsweek*, June 28, 2008, p. 2. www.newsweek.com/id/143 701/page/2.

9. Quoted in *Environmental Finance*, "All but One Product Fail Greenwashing Survey," November 22, 2007. www.environ mental-finance.com/onlinews/1122gre.html.

10. Quoted in Ellison, "Save the Planet, Lose the Guilt," p. 4.

11. Ben Elgin, "Another Inconvenient Truth," *BusinessWeek*, March 26, 2007. www.businessweek.com/magazine/content/07_13/b4027057.htm.

12. Quoted in Elgin, "Another Inconvenient Truth."

Chapter 2: Green on the Go

13. Ellen McRae, personal correspondence by phone and e-mail, July 12 and July 19, 2008.

14. Quoted in Larry Copeland, "Healthy Alternative: Take Mass Transit," *USA Today*, January 31, 2008. www.usatoday.com/news/nation/2008-01-31-masstransit_N.htm.

15. Tommy Lewis Tilden, "Hollywood's Hot Oscar Week: Going Green," Daily Green, February 25, 2008. www.thedailygreen.com/living-green/blogs/celebrities/hollywood-oscar-week-460225.

16. Virginia Miller, "Metro Riders Are Reminded of Their 'Sweet' Contribution to a Healthy Environment by Taking Public Transportation on Earth Day," American Public Transportation Association, News Release, April 21, 2008. www.apta.com/media/releases/080421_carbon.cfm.

17. P. J. O'Rourke, "Mass Transit Hysteria: Take the Plunge, Save the Planet," *Wall Street Journal*, March 16, 2005. www.opinionjournal.com/editorial/feature.html?id=110006428.

18. Erin Courtenay, "Julia Roberts Gets on the Bus," TreeHugger, July 24, 2006. www.treehugger.com/files/2006/07/julia_roberts_g.php.

19. Quoted in Hydrogen Cars & Vehicles, "Yellow Taxis Going Green with Propane," March 18, 2008. www.hydrogencarsnow.com/blog2/index.php/competition/yellow-taxis-going-green-with-propane.

20. Quoted in Virginia Miller, "Make Earth Day Your Transportation Day," American Public Transportation Association, News Release, April 16, 2008. www.apta.com/media/releases/080416_earth_day.cfm.

21. Tom Mutchler, "Not Always Keen Going Green: Honda Civic GX," *Consumer Reports*, February 14, 2008. http://blogs.consumerreports.org/cars/2008/02/honda-civic-gx.html.

22. Ellison, "Save the Planet, Lose the Guilt."

23. Quoted in Sholnn Freeman, "Boomers' New Ride: The Middle-Aged Are Going Green, and Automakers Follow," *Washington Post*, February 25, 2007. www.washingtonpost.com/wp-dyn/content/article/2007/02/24/AR2007022400099.html.

24. Elizabeth Rogers and Thomas M. Kostigen, *The Green Book: The Everyday Guide to Saving the Planet One Simple Step at a Time*. New York: Three Rivers Press, 2007, p. 86.

25. Keith Naughton, "Is There a Hybrid Auto in Your Future?" *Newsweek*, July 7/July 14, 2008, p. 54.

26. Naughton, "Is There a Hybrid Auto in Your Future?" p. 54.

27. *Washington Post*, "Half Gas, Half Electric, Totally California Cool," June 6, 2002, p. C01.

28. Ron Cogan, "Perspective: Daimler Creates a Practical Fuel Cell Minivan," GreenCar.com. www.greencar.com/perspective/necar-2-fuel-cell.

29. Sophie Uliano, *Gorgeously Green: 8 Simple Steps to an Eco-Friendly Life*. New York: HarperCollins, 2008, p. 251.

30. Uliano, *Gorgeously Green*, p. 251.

31. Quoted in Ellison, "Save the Planet, Lose the Guilt."

Chapter 3: The Green House

32. *BusinessWeek*, "The Greenest House on the Planet," September 11, 2006. www.businessweek.com/magazine/content/06_37/b4000079.htm.

33. Quoted in Amanda Griscom, "Who's the Greenest of Them All?" *Grist*, November 25, 2003. www.grist.org/news/powers/2003/11/25/of/.

34. Quoted in PBS, "Eco-Friendly Buildings," Online NewsHour, April 15, 2005. www.pbs.org/newshour/bb/environment/jan-june05/building_4-15.html.

35. Quoted in Matt Woolsey, "Nine Earth-Friendly Fixes for Your Home," *Forbes*, April 14, 2008. www.forbes.com/2008/04/14/green-home-energy-forbeslife-cx_mw_0414realestate.html.

36. *Environmental Building News*, "Green Building Materials: What Makes a Product Green?" Special Reprint, January 2006, p. 2.

37. Daylighting Collaborative, "What/Why: Ten Daylighting Myths—Unclouded." www.daylighting.org/what.php.

38. Quoted in David Bach, with Hillary Rosner, *Go Green, Live Rich: 50 Simple Ways to Save the Earth and Get Rich Trying*. New York: Broadway Books, 2008, p. 38.

39. Quoted in Griscom, "Who's the Greenest of Them All?"

40. Quoted in Rob Fanjoy, "Busted! Eight Green Building Myths," HGTVpro.com. www.hgtvpropicks.com/hpro/nws_ind_nws_ trends/article/0,2624,HPRO_26519_4953809_02,00.html.

Chapter 4: Shopping Green

41. Quoted in Carole Marie Cropper, "Does It Pay to Buy Organic?" *BusinessWeek*, September 6, 2004, www.businessweek .com/magazine/content/04_36/b3898129_mz070.htm.

42. Quoted in Singer, "Natural, Organic Beauty," p. 1.

43. Quoted in Singer, "Natural, Organic Beauty," p. 2

44. Quoted in Kara DiMillo, "Patagonia Celebrates 10 Years of Organic," TreeHugger, October 4, 2006. www.treehugger .com/files/2006/10/patagonia_celeb_1.php.

45. Quoted in Josh Dorfman, *The Lazy Environmentalist: Your Guide to Easy, Stylish, Green Living*. New York: Stewart, Tabori & Chang, 2007, p. 123.

46. Beth Terry, "Dear (*Blue Vinyl* DVD Distributor) New Video," Fake Plastic Fish, May 13, 2008. www.fakeplasticfish .com/2008/05/dear-blue-vinyl-dvd-distributor-new.html.

47. Quoted in Mike Cezilic, "Edward Norton Offers Earth-Friendly Advice," *Today*, April 22, 2008. www.msnbc.msn .com/id/24257539.

48. Quoted in Rogers and Kostigen, *The Green Book*, p. 13.

49. Miguel Llanos, "Ready to Rethink Toilet Paper for Earth Day?" MSNBC, April 21, 2006. www.msnbc.msn.com/id/12318915.

50. Natural Living for Women, "New Choices in Recycled Items." www.natural-living-for-women.com/recycled-products.html.

Chapter 5: Reduce, Reuse, Recycle

51. William McDonough and Michael Braungart, *Cradle to Cradle: Remaking the Way We Make Things*. New York: North Point Press, 2002, p. 28.

52. Quoted in Kenneth R. Weiss, "Plague of Plastic Chokes the Seas," *Los Angeles Times*, August 2, 2006. www.latimes.com/ news/local/oceans/la-me-ocean2aug02,0,3130914.story.

53. eNewsUSA, "Markey Introduces Bottle Recycling Climate Protection Act," November 17, 2007. http://enewsusa.blogspot .com/2007/11/markey-introduces-bottle-deposit.html.

54. Elizabeth Royte, *Garbage Land: On the Secret Trail of Trash*. New York: Little, Brown, 2005, p. 136.

55. Quoted in Royte, *Garbage Land*, p. 137.

56. Richard C. Porter, *The Economics of Waste*, Washington, DC: RFF Press, 2002, p. 12.

57. Quoted in Michael Munger, "Think Globally, Act Irrationally: Recycling," Library of Economics and Liberty. http://econlib.org/library/Columns/y2007/Mungerrecycling.html.

58. Munger, "Think Globally, Act Irrationally: Recycling."

59. Quoted in Royte, *Garbage Land*, p. 189.

60. Quoted in Talia Buford, "Cox's Compost Channel," *Providence Journal*, June 11, 2008. www.projo.com/news/environment/content/WB_WW_COX_RECYCLES_06-11-08_I4ACQ8T_v18.37356bb.html.

61. Quoted in Buford, "Cox's Compost Channel."

62. Joan D. Filsinger, "Worm Composting: Wriggling Recyclers Transform Kitchen Scraps into Compost," *Fine Gardening*, July/August 1997, p. 30.

63. Quoted in Karyn Ostrom, "Worm Bin Composting Draws Greater Interest," *Bronx Beat*, May 2, 2008. www.bronxbeat.org/cs/ContentServer?childpagename=Bronxbeat08%2FJRN_Content_C%2FRW1StoryDetailLayout2&c=JRN_Content_C&pagename=JRN%2FRW1Wrapper&cid=1175374771403&site=Bronxbeat08.

64. Quoted in Ostrom, "Worm Bin Composting Draws Greater Interest."

65. Quoted in Royte, *Garbage Land*, p. 115.

66. Quoted in Royte, *Garbage Land*, p. 114.

67. James I. Miller, "Municipal Composting Gains Acceptance; Provides Relief for Landfills," *American Recycler*, May 2004. www.americanrecycler.com/0504municipal.shtml.

68. Quotations Page, "Margaret Mead." www.quotationspage.com/quote/33522.html.

69. Uliano, *Gorgeously Green*, p. xv.

DISCUSSION QUESTIONS

Chapter 1: Why Green?

1. Explain some reasons other than going green that people might buy hybrid cars or energy-saving appliances.

2. How have local governments and businesses made it easier to go green?

3. What is greenwashing? Why do manufacturers engage in greenwashing?

4. What is an environmental trade-off? Give an example.

5. What is carbon offsetting? How does it work?

Chapter 2: Green on the Go

1. What is our carbon footprint?

2. Why is riding public transportation "one of the most powerful weapons" for combating global climate change?

3. What are biofuels?

4. How does a hybrid engine work?

5. What are the main advantages and disadvantages of electric vehicles?

Chapter 3: The Green House

1. How can the location and siting of a building affect the resources it will consume?

2. What factors do green builders consider when selecting building materials?

3. Why is daylighting considered a green practice?

4. How can people live "off the grid"?

5. Describe some water conservation strategies.

6. Why is natural landscaping usually better than planting shrubs or trees grown in other parts of the country?

Chapter 4: Shopping Green

1. Why are organic food, clothing, and health-care products considered green?

2. Why do organic products sometimes cost more?

3. Are organic or natural products always better for you? Why or why not?

4. Why do green consumers avoid plastic toys and packaging?

Chapter 5: Reduce, Reuse, Recycle

1. How does reusing something differ from recycling it?

2. What are some of the main obstacles to recycling paper, glass, aluminum cans, plastic bags, and other products?

3. What is composting? What types of waste can be composted?

ORGANIZATIONS TO CONTACT

Action For Nature
2269 Chestnut Street, #263
San Francisco, CA 94123
phone: (415) 421-2640
e-mail: mail@actionfornature.org
Web site: www.actionfornature.org

Action For Nature is a U.S.-based nonprofit organization that inspires young people to take action for the environment and protect the natural world in their own neighborhood and around the world. The group's International Young Eco-Heroes Awards Program recognizes children and teens who have completed projects to foster respect and affection for nature through personal action.

Alliance to Save Energy
1850 M Street NW, Suite 600
Washington, DC 20036
phone: (202) 857-0666
e-mail: info@ase.org
Web site: www.ase.org

The Alliance to Save Energy promotes energy efficiency worldwide to achieve a healthier economy, a cleaner environment, and greater energy security. Its programs include Green Schools and Green Campus Programs, which are designed to engage students in encouraging energy efficiency and conservation.

Earth Day Network (EDN)
1616 P Street NW, Suite 340
Washington, DC 20036
phone: (202) 518-0044
Web site: www.earthday.net

The Earth Day Network grew out of the original Earth Day in 1970. EDN's international network reaches more than seventeen thousand organizations in 174 countries and seeks to grow, diversify, and mobilize the environmental movement worldwide through education, politics, events, and consumer activism.

The Environmental Literacy Council
1625 K Street NW, Suite 1020
Washington, DC 20006
phone: (202) 296-0390
e-mail: info@enviroliteracy.org
Web site: www.enviroliteracy.org

The Environmental Literacy Council is a nonprofit environmental organization composed of scientists, economists, and educators striving to connect teachers and students to science-based information on environmental issues such as energy use, climate change, and recycling.

Environmental Resources Center
University of Wisconsin
445 Henry Mall, Room 202
Madison, WI 53706
phone: (608) 262-0020
Web site: www.uwex.edu/erc

Based at the University of Wisconsin, the Environmental Resources Center provides research, education, and resources on a wide range of environmental issues.

National Audubon Society
225 Varick Street, 7th Floor
New York, NY 10014
phone: (212) 979-3000
Web site: www.audubonathome.org

The mission of the National Audubon Society is to conserve and restore natural ecosystems, focusing on birds and other wildlife. The nonprofit organization provides scientific, advocacy, and educational programs, engaging millions of people of all ages and backgrounds in positive conservation experiences.

National Environmental Education Foundation
4301 Connecticut Ave. NW, Suite 160
Washington, DC 20008
phone: (202) 833-2933
Web site: www.neefusa.org

The National Environmental Education Foundation was chartered by Congress in 1990 to advance environmental knowledge and action with the ultimate goal of promoting environmentally responsible behavior in the general public. The foundation provides objective environmental information to help Americans live better every day.

U.S. Department of Energy
1000 Independence Ave. SW
Washington, DC 20585
phone: (800) 342-5363
Web site: www.doe.gov

The U.S. Department of Energy provides information about energy efficiency and alternative sources of energy. The department's WaterSense Program also has information on water conservation tools and techniques that everyone can use.

U.S. Environmental Protection Agency
Ariel Rios Building
1200 Pennsylvania Ave. NW
Washington, DC 20460
phone: (202) 272-0167
Web site: www.epa.gov

Created in 1970, the Environmental Protection Agency is the primary federal agency charged with protecting human health and the environment. In addition to enforcing environmental laws and regulations, the EPA performs environmental research and advances environmental education.

U.S. Green Building Council
1800 Massachusetts Ave. NW, Suite 300
Washington, DC 20036
phone: (800) 795-1747
e-mail: info@usgbc.org
Web site: www.usgbc.org

The U.S. Green Building Council is a nonprofit organization that provides a wealth of information about building green homes, schools, and commercial buildings, including the Leadership in Environmental and Energy Design (LEED) certification program.

Books

David Bach, with Hillary Rosner, *Go Green, Live Rich: 50 Simple Ways to Save the Earth and Get Rich Trying*. New York: Broadway Books, 2008. This beautifully illustrated book provides fifty ideas for going green that also help save money.

Tristan Boyer Binns, *Clean Planet: Stopping Litter and Pollution*. Chicago: Heinemann Library, 2005. This book is based on the premise that people cause most of the pollution in our world, that no one is "safe" from pollution, and that everyone can make a difference in cleaning it up. The book discusses how people can make a difference in the environmental health of their communities and of the planet as a whole.

Eleanor J. Hall, *Recycling*. Detroit: KidHaven Press, 2005. This book introduces readers to the benefits and challenges of recycling newspapers, glass, plastics, and other household materials.

Kris Hirschmann, *Going Green*. Yankton, SD: Erickson Press, 2008. This easy reader provides an overview of the green movement and what people are doing at home and in their communities to protect the environment.

Carol Inskipp, *Reducing and Recycling Waste*. Milwaukee, WI: Gareth Stevens, 2005. This book emphasizes the importance of acting now if we are to preserve our natural resources for ourselves and future generations, describes the causes and effects of problems around the globe, and offers helpful suggestions for reducing and recycling waste.

Yvonne Jeffery, Michael Grosvenor, and Liz Barclay, *Green Living for Dummies*. Indianapolis: Wiley, 2008. This book offers hundreds of ideas for making environmentally responsible decisions, from simple suggestions like shutting off appliances and water when they are not being used, to purchasing with "green" in mind, to craft projects for reusing common household items.

Elizabeth Rogers and Thomas M. Kostigen, *The Green Book: The Everyday Guide to Saving the Planet One Simple Step at a Time*. New York: Three Rivers Press, 2007. This book provides simple steps for becoming more environmentally friendly and why what we do matters to the planet. The book also provides stories about what some famous people are doing to help protect the environment.

Louise Spilsbury, *Environment at Risk: The Effects of Pollution*. Chicago: Raintree, 2006. This book focuses on how people and pollution affect the earth. It discusses many key environmental issues facing our earth today, including global warming, acid rain, air and water pollution, and the use—and overuse—of nonrenewable resources.

Charlotte Wilcox, *Recycling*, Minneapolis, MN: Lerner, 2007. This book focuses on the science of recycling and explains the many amazing ways people use science to turn garbage into great things.

Web Sites

Clean Sweep U.S.A. (www.cleansweepusa.org). Hosted by the nonprofit environmental group Keep America Beautiful, this Web site offers information, games, and lessons about waste management, recycling, composting, and a host of related issues.

The Consumer's Handbook for Reducing Solid Waste (www.epa.gov/epaoswer/non-hw/reduce/catbook/index.htm). This site describes how people can help solve a growing problem—garbage!

EcoKids (www.ecokidsonline.com). This Canadian Web site provides information about the environment and offers games and activities where you can test your knowledge about the environment and your impact upon it.

EEK! Our Earth (www.dnr.state.wi.us/org/caer/ce/eek/earth/index.htm). This lively and engaging Web site, hosted by the Wisconsin Department of Natural Resources, offers a wealth of information about the environment and how to protect it.

Environmental Literacy Council (www.enviroliteracy.org). The Environmental Literacy Council is dedicated to helping students understand environmental issues. Its comprehensive Web site contains resources on almost every aspect of the natural world.

EPA Student Center (www.epa.gov/students). This site, hosted by the U.S. Environmental Protection Agency, provides a host of activities and resources for teachers and students of all ages, including information on environmental basics, recycling, and conservation.

Going Green (www.geocities.com/RainForest/Vines/4990). This earth-friendly site offers tips that people young and old can implement in their households, schools, or communities to save our planet, as well as a list of books and links to other environmental Web sites.

Recycle City (www.epa.gov/recyclecity). There are lots of people and places to visit and plenty of interactive games to explore how Recycle City's residents recycle, reduce, and reuse waste.

INDEX

PICTURE CREDITS

Cover image: Image copyright ZQFotography, 2009. Used under license from Shutterstock.com

Maury Aaseng, 91

AP Images, 7, 9, 14, 15, 17, 23, 25, 30, 34, 36, 39, 42, 44, 46, 48, 51, 55, 61, 62, 64, 66, 69, 71, 77, 78, 81, 83, 85, 87, 94, 96, 98, 100

AP Photo/The Plain Dealer, John Kuntz, 11

Don Emmert/AFP/Getty Images, 35

Cate Gillon/Getty Images, 74

Lawrence Bender Prods./The Kobal Collection/Lee, Eric, 20

Scott Olson/Getty Images, 89

Mark Thomson/The Christian Science Monitor/Getty Images, 59

Dougal Waters/Photodisc/Getty Images, 21

ABOUT THE AUTHOR

Lydia Bjornlund is a freelance writer in northern Virginia, where she lives with her husband, Gerry Hoetmer, and their wonderful children, Jake and Sophia. She has written more than a dozen nonfiction books for children, mostly on American history and health-related topics. She also writes books and training materials for adults on issues related to conservation and public management. Lydia holds a master's degree in education from Harvard University and a BA from Williams College.